Indexing Biographies

and Other Stories of Human Lives

T0338994

Indexing Biographies

and Other Stories of Human Lives

Fourth edition

HAZEL K. BELL

LIVERPOOL UNIVERSITY PRESS

First edition published 1992
Second edition published 1998
Third edition published 2004

This fourth edition published 2020 by
Liverpool University Press
4 Cambridge Street
Liverpool L69 7ZU, UK
www.liverpooluniversitypress.co.uk

ISBN 978-1-78962-162-4 (limp)
Typeset by Carnegie Book Production, Lancaster
Printed and bound in Poland by BooksFactory.co.uk

Contents

Acknowledgements

We acknowledge with thanks permission granted by all the authors of articles or publishers of indexes quoted herein to reproduce those passages, and by Peters, Fraser and Dunlop in respect of extracts from the index to Pepys' diary.

Excerpts from *Nineteen Eighty-four* by George Orwell, copyright 1949 by Harcourt Brace & Company and renewed 1977 by Sonia Brownell Orwell, reprinted by permission of the publisher, of Mark Hamilton, the Literary Executor of the Estate of the Late Sonia Brownell Orwell, and Martin Secker & Warburg Ltd.

1. Narrative texts and stories of lives

'Soft' texts

Stories of human lives are recounted in histories, biographies, autobiographies, diaries – also in fiction; always in narrative form, distinct from documentary texts. Such stories bring particular problems for indexers, with regard both to form and content.

The indexer of the humanities – literary or biographical works; books basically about people and their personal experiences – is often dealing with accounts of personal relationships and emotions rather than with documentary facts: what I would call 'soft texts', expressed in flexible, literary language. The indexer of these has to make assessments of the selection of items to index, and the terms in which to express them, on the basis of subjective value judgement, being, as Douglas Matthews puts it, 'in a sense, an interpreter, not just a reporter of the text' (Matthews, personal communication, 1991).

Human lives are generally not lived in accordance with strict principles, and irregularities in lives that are being indexed must be met by flexible indexing practice, with index entries selected not uniformly according to specifiable categories, but by individual degree of significance, as assessed by the indexer, who is gauging the calibre of references rather than their kind (Bell, 1991a, b). Each biography tells a unique story: Alain de Botton refers to 'the extraordinariness of any life, a singularity' (de Botton, 1995).

What I call 'soft' texts have been distinguished from documentary ones previously under other terms. Most largely, they reflect the difference drawn by Richard Abel between information (dry) and knowledge (soft):

> The way in which *knowledge,* once created, is stored and retrieved distinguishes this form of intellectual activity from that of the

discovery of *information*. The latter is readily stored, not only in journal papers, but also in computer databases. Information can be stored in these ways due to its discrete, particular, specific and quantitative qualities. Knowledge, by contrast, is only partly quantitative. It is discursive, general and broad-ranging with only very indistinct boundaries. (Abel, 1991)

The narrative form

The narrative (historical) form was differentiated from that of 'documentary texts' by Cecelia Wittmann (Wittmann, 1990). By documentary texts we understand collections of discrete, self-contained units: articles, essays, lectures, brochures, works, documents in general, which usually may be indexed item by item. Narrative texts, by contrast, sustain their threads continuously through the whole work, not broken into separate units, but extending through entire volumes or sequences of volumes. Chapter endings are pauses in a continuing story, not changes of topic. Whole narrative works contain recurrent characters and themes whose constant development must be kept in mind throughout the whole, not just dealt with and dismissed from the sequence.

The extended continuity of a complete narrative entails large numbers of references building up for the major topics, so that subdivision and specification of many references will become necessary: narrative indexers must analyse and rephrase their texts closely. Hans Wellisch describes narrative indexing as 'providing the user with the context of an indexed item' (Wellisch, 1991). These present the indexer of soft texts with the problem of sustained continuity, the constant development of characters and themes. Much subdivision and specification will become necessary, with the devising of appropriate subheadings.

Gordon Carey, the first President of the Society of Indexers, who compiled the indexes of over sixty books, including the autobiographies of Lords Attlee, Brabazon, Ismay and Maugham, and a biography of Lord Haldane, wrote, 'The compilation of entries loaded with subheadings is, to my mind, the task that calls for the indexer's highest skill of all' (Carey, 1961).

As narrative texts deal with human lives, which have never been standardized, there are few rules and standards specifically for indexing these; such indexing must be individual and subjective.

Sensitive content

The indexer of human lives may also have particular problems to cope with regarding the matter in hand, contending with sensitive humanitarian aspects of anatomizing psyche. We may feel guilty of invading privacy, or causing distress by what we draw attention to. Roger Cooper's book about his experiences as a hostage in Lebanon, *Death plus ten years*, was published by HarperCollins without an index. Asked to explain the lack, they replied:

> We took the deliberate decision not to include an index for the simple reason that the book is a personal account of a very harrowing experience, and that, as such, it becomes somewhat otiose to have to include an enormous entry detailing Roger's every thought or action. It's the kind of book which deserves re-reading, in its entirety perhaps. (personal communication)

Indexers may still have to bite the sensitive bullet. The personal accounts of their hostage experiences by John McCarthy, Terry Anderson, and Terry Waite all appeared with detailed indexes. Indexing a history of the Resistance movement in World War II, based on newly accessible records, I was horribly aware that the relatives of Gestapo victims might learn here for the first time the exact, awful details of their fates. Indexing the love letters of a mystic poet, intended for no third eye, let alone publication, made me feel a most intrusive voyeur as I sought to reduce outpourings of spiritual ecstasy to precise terms (Bushrui, 1980).

Sometimes it seems cruel to deal a double blow, reinforcing in the index the exposure or censure of folly or wrongdoing in the text. We worry too as to whether we may be held guilty as accessories to libel in indicating where scurrilous allegations are to be found. Envying both the impersonality and standardization of documentary indexing, the soft indexers of human lives search their souls as well as their thesauri.

We who take human lives in our hands, in the words of Paul Barnett, 'beyond the appendix with gun and camera' (Barnett, 1983), have heavy responsibilities as well as a heavy task.

History

Histories are usually narrative texts, with biographies occurring within them.

Indexers of histories have certain advantages over the indexers of biographies. Much of their subject in hand – the period, its events, and public figures – will be known to them: subject expertise applies here. They are also able to imply much in a simple date specification (such as 1066 or 1914–18) without having to explain its significance to the text in a gloss. For events that have been frequently recounted – and indexed – standard descriptive labels may well have become established that can be used as subheadings, so there are published precedents available to consult.

Examining histories indexed by their authors, Piggott suggested criteria for indexers of histories:

> Both our historians thought chronologically, were scrupulously exact in presenting names and in distinguishing between separate instances of the same phenomenon [...] both strove to fulfill the requirements of scholarship in accurate statement and citation. (Piggott, 1991)

The indexing of local and family history has particular requirements, as claimed by Bob Trubshaw:

> Whereas in most books there would be little point in indexing minor mentions of individuals, buildings and street names, this would be very frustrating for local and family history researchers because it is just such 'trivial' aspects that they are often most keen to track down, or which are the only clues to locating more relevant information. (Trubshaw, 2005)

Articles on the indexing of **narrative history** that have appeared in *The Indexer* are:

Bias in indexing [on Laurence Echard/John Oldmixon]. Margaret Anderson. **9**(1), 27–30

Twenty-five years of history indexing: a practitioner's report. E. H. Boehm. **11**(1), 33–42

The indexing work of Family History Societies. J. S. W. Gibson. **13**(2), 83–5

Indexes for local and family history: a user's view. John Chandler. **13**(4), 223–7

Indexing ancient history. R. D. Rodriguez. **14**(3), 207–8

User approaches to indexes [family history]. Jean Stirk. **16**(2), 75–8

Observations on the indexing of history: the example of the *Journal of American History*. M. B. Gilmore. **16**(3), 159–62

Authors as their own indexers [Elizabethan England]. Mary Piggott. **17**(3), 161–6

'Discursive, dispersed, heterogeneous': indexing *Seven pillars of wisdom*. Hazel K. Bell. **24**(1), 9–11

'A funny lot': indexing and local history books. Bob Trubshaw. **24**(4), 184–5

Christian history: 3,000 years and an author's indexing thereof. Diarmaid MacCulloch. **28**(2), 108–9

History indexes reviewed. Catherine Sassen. **31**(3), 105–9

Working with Hannibal and the Folio Society. Gerard M-F. Hill. **31**(4), 173

So many words: indexing oral history. Mary Newberry et al. **34**(4), 144–7

Biography

Philip Hensher provides us with a useful definition of an index to a biography (Hensher, 2004):

> If a biography is a reduction of a life's experiences to the span of a single volume, then the index is a further reduction, indicating

the general characteristics, of recurrent themes, of the bare truth which a book cloaks in prose.

Richard Abel may gladden our hearts with:

> Biographies and autobiographies, when composed, published and sold in keeping with the traditional canons of sound judgement, have been, and remain, among the crown jewels of the book trade. (Abel, 1993)

And '[t]he fascination of reading biographies is irresistible', wrote Virginia Woolf (Woolf, 1932). But less respect is paid to their indexes. At the Society of Indexers' conference in Cheltenham, 1988, a voice was raised to declare scornfully in a discussion session, 'Surely anyone can index a biography!'. Contemptuously addressing those indexers he regarded as lacking professionalism, John Simkin wrote in *The Indexer*: 'If all you've ever bothered to learn is how to knock off an index to a book on some well-known topic – gardening, biography, cookery...' (Simkin, 1997). Such disparagements are not uncommon: alas, indexing biographies is not a subject specialism, and lacks the respect accorded those.

Special subjects consist of bodies of lore of academic disciplines, established facts. They may be provided with standardized terminology and formalized structure for their texts. Biographies involve none of these, being just books about people, the lives they lead, their various activities and relationships, told in an author's own way. They are non-standardized.

Indexers are frequently cautioned that they should never index a book on a subject not within their specialist knowledge. Indexers of biographies, though, are all too often called upon to do just that. Biographies may be the first on their newly discovered or newly famed subjects, may contain whole new areas of information, or aim to give new knowledge about the lives of their subjects. The main characters are likely to live among people not well known. No one would claim detailed knowledge of all lives lived and likely to be recorded in print: biographical indexers may well be working on unfamiliar topics, making no claim to expertise. Biography is a genre, not a subject specialism.

However, subject specialisms of several sorts may yet come to be desired, as our heroes enter and practise their various careers. I have undertaken the indexing of biographies of Leonardo da Vinci and of Lawrence of Arabia. What subject specialist could one recommend to cover the whole extraordinary career of either of those polymaths? Contrariwise, several scientific indexers have told me how, when they were asked to index biographies of their disciplines' heroes, they found themselves at a loss as to how to proceed. Caroline Barlow riposted to Simkins' sneer quoted above, 'As a scientist I usually steer clear of biographies for the reason that you don't know what subject range (usually large) they will contain' (Barlow, 1998).

Disregarded indexers of biographies may, however, relish Giles Gordon's description of *Oscar Wilde* by Richard Ellmann as '846-page (including notes and index, essential to any self-regarding biographer)' (Gordon, 1993). Less laudable advocacy for biographical indexes:

> There have been few biographies in the past half-century that have come to fewer than 600 pages [...] For an ordinary newspaper reviewer, for instance, it means that a biography should have a good index to help him skip perhaps half a thousand pages. Biography, especially governance biography, now has to be designed for skippage. (Whittemore, 1999)

Certainly, any account of an entire life may grow mighty long, extending through several volumes. Charles Moore's *Margaret Thatcher: the authorised biography*, vol. 1 alone (Penguin, 2013) was hailed by a reviewer as 'a doorstop biography' (Johnson, 2014). Brian Sewell, reviewing *Van Gogh: the life*, by S. Naifeh and G. White Smith (Profile, 2011) with 912 pp., commented: 'It is a worthy but not worthwhile effort, for who now has the time to read a thousand pages crammed with uncomfortably small print? [...] its index is invaluable for finding odd facts not easily discoverable elsewhere' (Sewell, 2012).

Articles on the **general indexing of biographies** that have appeared in *The Indexer* are:

No room at the top. G. V. Carey. **2**(4), 120–3

A list of literary figures featured in *The Indexer* can be found in 'Contents by category' on its website, at https://www.theindexer.org/indexes/contents-by-category/.

Autobiography

Indexers of autobiographies may have an easier task than those indexing third-person accounts of others' lives. In 'A sketch of the past' Virginia Woolf noticed how often memoirs 'leave out the person to whom things happened', since events are easier to describe than the person they happen to (Woolf, 1939). As G. V. Carey wrote of indexing a volume of memoirs, 'Not unnaturally, the author did not expatiate on his own personality' (Carey, 1961). And how often is the author of an autobiography also its indexer? Indexing the main character, oneself, in a first-person narrative would seem a Lacanian distinction of Self and Other. The indication of much character analysis may be spared the indexer of autobiography.

Treatment of the main character in a biography constitutes one of the main problems of its indexing (see chapter 9), but the narrators of texts themselves rarely occupy the foreground, and where the narrator is also the protagonist they may appear less prominent, their own activities and characteristics less demanding of constant specification. Autobiographers, unless unduly egotistical, tend to write more of those they observe and encounter than of themselves. (For an egotistical example, see the eulogistic subheadings in the entry for Joseph Bonanno in his autobiography – discussed in Chapter 6.)

Autobiography may take several forms, including memoirs, journals, and diaries.

Political memoirs

Alan Walker observes:

> Two features make 'political memoirs' a special class of writing: that they are autobiography rather than biography, and that they are a species of political discourse. (Walker, 2012b)

Impartiality (see chapter 6) is surely most necessary here. Staunch Whig Lord Macaulay famously realised this, crying 'Let no damned Tory index my book!'. But hostility appears in political memoirs nevertheless. The authors of these two seem to come to virtual blows in their indexes:

> I turn to the index – which, as everyone knows, is the only part of books by politicians anyone ever reads with interest – of John Redwood's *Singing the Blues: The Once and Future Conservatives.* Major, John, begins a hefty section, characteristic equivocation of; and difficulties with election promises; discourages sensible debate in Cabinet; [...] foolish decisions of; lets down people; makes claims in memoirs; makes right decision to resign; [...] takes wrong course of action over Maastrich. Oh dear. *Honi soit qui mal y pense,* pointy ears. When we turn to the index of Mr Major's autobiography, what do we find? Redwood, John: Citizen's Charter; assumed to be disloyal. (*The Questing Vole, The Spectator,* 16 October 2004)

The characters featured in such memoirs may well still be living, and constitute an eager – or anxious – potential readership. Walker records that the launch of *John Howard: Lazarus rising* (HarperCollins Sydney, 2010), a political autobiography that he indexed, 'was like a walking index' (Walker, 2012a).

But the very relevance of the political memoir to so many potential readers may even lead to publication *sans* index. In 2004 *The Indexer* featured 'the Washington read', quoting Richard Ben Cramer explaining why his 1000-page account of the 1988 US presidential campaign, *What it takes: the way to the White House* (Vintage Books, 1992) was published without an index (Fox, 2013):

> For years I watched all these Washington jerks, all these Capitol Hill, executive-branch, agency wise guys and reporters go into,

say, [a] bookstore, take a political book off the shelf, look up their names, glance at the page and put the book back. Washington reads by index, and I wanted those people to read the damn thing.

Articles on the **indexing of autobiographies** that have appeared in *The Indexer* are:

No room at the top [includes memoirs of Lord Ismay]. G. V. Carey. **2**(4), 120–3

Misrepresentation – *passim* [Joseph Bonanno]. Hazel K. Bell. **14**(1), 56

Authors as their own indexers [*1100 miles with Monty*]. Mary Piggott. **17**(3), 161–6

The 'Washington read' and the 'Clindex'. Christine Shuttleworth. **24**(2), 61

The Blair Index Project. Christine Shuttleworth. **28**(4), 175

Political memoirs: an international comparison of indexing styles. Alan Walker. **30**(2), 66–75

Indexing political memoirs: neutrality and partiality. Alan Walker. **30**(3), 125–30

Diaries

Karl Heumann reported that of his collection of 491 diaries and journals, 217 (44%) lacked an index. He claimed, 'a printed diary or journal without a proper index is a maimed thing and is not able to serve its full purpose even on a first reading' (Heumann, 1970).

According to Simon Brett, a diary may fulfil a variety of roles (Brett, 1987):

> It can be used to colour reality or to vent spleen. It can be a bald record of facts or a Gothic monument of prose. It can chart the conquests of a libertine or the seesawing emotions of a depressive. It can chronicle the aspirations of youth and the disillusionments of age. For a painter it can be a detailed notebook, for a writer an experimental canvas.

Diaries may pose peculiar difficulties for the indexer. Diary entries are more casually made than the writing of a formal autobiography, and seem to offer indexers less opportunity for the devising of meaningful subheadings. Not having been designed as narrative wholes for other readers, they are unlikely to introduce and explain their recurrent characters, who will probably have large numbers of minor, background references – in lists of those making up groups and parties, for example.

Perhaps *passim* may be allowable for diaries, indicating minor mentions over a period of consecutive days.

Indexes to diaries tend to be fully glossed, to make up for the lack of initial description, and to have strings of page references not deserving special subheadings. The index to the published version of the diary of Barbara Pym is headed 'Index/Glossary' (Pym, 1985). The index to Lady Cynthia Asquith's *Diaries* includes these entries with only one page reference each (Asquith, 1968):

> Benson, Constance (d. 1946; wife of Frank Benson, the actor-manager who was knighted in 1916, but herself a somewhat indifferent performer), 259
>
> Broughton, Rhoda (1840–1920: novelist, author of *Not wisely but too well* pub. 1867, and others. Originally considered 'advanced' and shocking, she had been overtaken by time and respectability), 324

The entry for Cliffe, Polly, has ten lines of text and four lines of undifferentiated page numbers; that for McInnes, (Mrs) Angela has 15 lines of text with two page numbers. The index includes a typographic novelty in one entry:

> Douglas, Lord Alfred (1870–1945: son of the 8th Marquess of Queensberry. His relationship with Lady Cynthia was as follows: [a small family tree is reproduced in the index at this point]

Hugh Muir observes of Alastair Campbell's diaries (Arrow, 2012):

> from [the index] you get an instant view of Alastair's impatience with Clare Short. 'Ghastly to deal with', 89; ridiculous in Cabinet, 256; spills tea over new Cabinet Secretary, 307; 'totally ridiculous', 331; interruptions worse than usual, 348; exacerbates problems, 544, 548, 550.' The text is superfluous really. (Muir, 2012)

Much praise has been accorded to the indexes to E. S. de Beer's edition of John Evelyn's *Diary* (in six volumes), and indexes to the diaries of Samuel Pepys and William Gladstone have won the Wheatley Medal – see below, chapter 2.

Articles on *the indexing of diaries* that have appeared in *The Indexer* are:

> Indexing **Pepys's** diary. Robert and Rosalind Latham. **12**(1), 34–5
> 'The index to the definitive **Pepys'**. Robert Latham. **14**(2), 88–90
> 'Thankless task' accomplished (for **Barbara Pym**). Hazel K. Bell. **14**(3), 189
> A glossy index (Lady Cynthia **Asquith's** *Diaries*). Hazel K. Bell. **18**(1), 47
> Indexing **Gladstone**: from 5 x 3" cards to computer and database. H. C. G. Matthew. **19**(4), 257–64
> Indexing Wesley's journals and diaries. John A. **Vickers**. **25**(1), 9–11
> 'And so to bed': the index to The diary of Samuel **Pepys**. Fred Leise. **29**(1), 4–11

Letters

Although written in discrete, not narrative form, and 'for the moment; their function is individual, not sequential or cumulative; they normally involve a variety of recipients' (Barnes, 2000), sequences of letters may acquire a sense of continuity, developing events and lives. Julian Barnes, indeed, suggests, in the case of Gustave Flaubert, that 'the *Correspondance* has always added up to Flaubert's best biography', commenting, 'This is the advantage of letters over biography: letters exist in real time. We read them at about the speed at which they were written. Biography gives us the crane-shot, the time-elision, the astute selectivity' (Barnes, 2000). It is therefore appropriate to consider the indexing of collections of letters (which may extend through several volumes), and its peculiar difficulties, here.

The letters of authors may have a triple manifestation: as literary works themselves, published or fit to be published; aspects of relationships described in the biography; and sources drawn on and cited by the biographer.

Books are usually written deliberately for publication – addressed to, structured and worded for, the general reader. Letters, though, are intended only for their first recipients, addressed deliberately to them, and so may well include references that third parties will not understand. Their sequence is chronological but not continuous; as narrative it may appear jerky, with omissions and perplexing references. In A. S. Byatt's novel, *Possession*, a character reflects: 'Letters [...] are a form of narrative that envisages no outcome, no closure. [...] Letters tell no story, because they do not know, from line to line, where they are going' (Byatt, 1990). As with diaries, themes will be dispersed in small bits, with reiterated minor references to people, causing strings of minor references to the same topics.

The dates at which people's names may be changed, or titles bestowed, cause difficulty for the indexer of volumes of letters. Jeremy Wilson, truly punctilious in matters of detail and authenticity, in his annotations to volumes of letters of T. E. Lawrence (Castle Press) '[tried] to ensure that the notes give the titles of people as they were at the time the letter was written'. He wanted the volumes' indexes to do the same, but realized that this would cause trouble in the cases where people were ennobled during Lawrence's lifetime, especially in the proposed cumulative index for all Castle Press works concerning Lawrence. He suggested that the index should contain entries such as 'Trenchard, Hugh (kt 1928)' (Wilson, personal communication, 2000).

Douglas Matthews addressed a Society of Indexers conference on 'the pleasures and pride derived from indexing volumes of published letters, and the particular challenges of the genre' (Matthews, 2001). He spoke of collections of letters as 'discrete and separate, cast in a variety of voices', liable to lay the indexer open to feelings of 'intrusiveness and embarrassment'; of the use of intimate names in correspondence; the possibility of a final cumulation of volume indexes; and the likelihood of having two related texts to cope with in indexing: the letters themselves, and the editor's notes and comments. Special techniques that he advocated were making a preliminary index of correspondents, and typographical distinction between correspondents in the general index and as recipients.

Indexes to volumes of letters have received high praise. The five-volume (3002-page) index to the 43 volumes of *The Yale edition of Horace Walpole's correspondence* (Oxford University Press, 1937–83), compiled by Warren Hunting Smith with three assistants, was reviewed thus in the *Times Literary Supplement*:

> The index is as meticulously thorough as human minds can contrive [...] All the letters are sifted and their contents classified in categories of astonishing detail. [...] typographical opulence, perhaps unique among indexes, helps to speed the skimming eye. [...] exemplary features [...] This great edition has been called encyclopaedic. Its index justifies that accolade. (Halsband, 1983)

Matthews' view of this index is in accordance. He writes, 'the cumulation stands by itself as a mighty accomplishment, and daunting to most of us. [...] This mighty work is one of elegant simplicity [...] Typographically it is very pleasing' (2001).

Matthews had many complimentary things to say too of James Thornton's indexes to Volume 2 (1840–1) of *The letters of Charles Dickens* (Clarendon Press, 1969; winner of the Wheatley Medal for that year), writing: 'The system he created is admirable, and he set high standards for treating these marvellous and extensive letters. There is a range of typographical devices for particular features' (Matthews, 2001).

G. Norman Knight also praised Thornton's indexes, singling out what he deemed 'a very useful innovation' (Knight, 1970):

> In a straight run of page numbers he would frequently identify a reference by inserting descriptive words, often quoted, in brackets after the page number; thus, under AMERICA: *Other references*, we have at the end: *also 87n, 104n, 108 ('great country'), 143 ('new World'), 405n, 429n*

Thornton himself wrote of R. W. Chapman's index to his edition of Samuel Johnson's *Letters*:

> Chapman champions the multiple index. [His] edition of Johnson's *Letters* in three volumes has seven classified indexes, which together occupy 135 pages of Volume III. He used his

indexes as a means of conveying to the reader a good deal of information of a kind that in other editions would find its way into the introduction or into an introductory note. The multiple index in this instance is therefore a valuable editorial device. (Thornton, 1968)

In both 2001 and 2002, the American Society of Indexers / H. W. Wilson Company Award, 'established to honor excellence in indexing [... and] to provide and publicize models of excellence in indexing' (American Society for Indexing) was awarded to indexers of collections of letters.

The 2001 award went to Ronald M. Gephart and Paul H. Smith for their cumulative index to *Letters of delegates to Congress, 1774–1789* (Library of Congress, 2000). The judging committee found that 'the cumulative index provides narrative analysis for the letters and makes the letters and history within accessible. As one judge said, "The index is the narrative"' (Wyman, 2001).

In 2002 the ASI award was won by Margie Towery for her cumulative index to *The Letters of Matthew Arnold* (six volumes; University Press of Virginia). The committee:

was impressed by the thoroughness of the index and its consequent usefulness to the scholars who are its primary audience. Towery's painstaking approach can be seen in the very precise page ranges given for each letter and the lists of 'mentioneds', the concise but elegant distinctions made between people with the same name, and the brief but clear analysis of the entries. The relevance and parallelism of the subheadings and the grammatical relationship between the subheads and the main headings are also outstanding. 'The language', as committee member Laura Gottlieb put it, 'is lovely'. All in all, the committee felt that this index not only provides excellent access to Arnold's letters, but stands as a shining example for anyone undertaking a similar project in the future'. (M. Anderson, 2002)

The ISC/SCI Ewart-Daveluy Award for Indexing Excellence was presented in 2016 to Mary Newberry for her index to the two-volume,

1,150-page, *Letterbooks of John Evelyn*, edited by Douglas D. C. Chambers and David Galbraith (University of Toronto Press). As the citation explains:

> Making this 1,150 letterbook material accessible to scholars was the job of the indexer, but it was not an easy job. The sheer volume of the material was one issue; another was the archaic diction and writing style of the seventeenth century. A third was the need to serve the scholars who were undoubtedly already familiar with de Beer's extensive index created for the 1955 publication of Evelyn's diaries and would expect some correlation, while also serving modern indexing standards and user expectations. Mary created a comprehensive index that demonstrates outstanding indexing expertise, analytical competence and index design skill. More than that, it exemplifies the index as a work of art.
> (Indexing society awards, 2016)

Articles on **indexing letters** that have appeared in *The Indexer* are:

How I indexed **Dickens**'s letters. J. Thornton. **4**(4), 119–22

On editing and indexing a series of letters [of **Sir Robert Hart**]. K. F. Bruner. **14**(1), 42–6

'A book very much to your credit': the index to the private edition of **Boswell**'s Papers. Judy Batchelor. **14**(2), 114

The **Burney** papers – or, where does an index begin? Althea Douglas, **14**(4), 241–8

Indexing published letters. Douglas Matthews. **22**(3), 135–41

After the Prize: indexing at the **Einstein** Papers Project. R. Hirschmann. **29**(2), 98–109

'Your letters have been life and breath to me': the challenge of indexing *My beloved man*' (letters of **Britten** and **Pears**). Marian Aird. **34**(4), 138–43

For the indexing of fiction, see chapter 14.

2. The great and good

We could look to the masterpieces of the indexing of life stories for models to examine and follow. Where are these to be found?

Indexing masterpieces

In *The Indexer* of Spring 1967 Esmond de Beer wrote the first of an intended series, 'Indexing masterpieces' (de Beer, 1967) devoted to L. F. Powell's index to his own six-volume revision of Boswell's *Life of Johnson* (Boswell, 1934–64). De Beer described this index as 'a most efficient and most appropriate complement to the text [...] The index reflects the conversable character of the book to which it is attached: one dips into it, dallies, falls a willing victim, looks up reference after reference.' Two full pages of the index are reproduced following the article: a page of the entry for Johnson himself, and the page running from Panckouke, Charles Joseph to Parentheses: a pound of them.

In his turn, de Beer himself received praise from Wheatley-winner (for his index to Pepys' diary) Robert Latham for his own 'superb index to the diary of John Evelyn with [...] its subtle refinements and almost inhuman accuracy' (Latham, 1984); 'It gives you a model to follow', he declared (Latham and Latham, 1980). De Beer was also the editor of this six-volume edition of Evelyn's diary (Oxford, 1955). Peter Laslett wrote in his obituary in *The Guardian* (Laslett, 1990):

> The 600 pages of the index volume to Evelyn's diary set a standard amongst the whole collection of books ever published in English. De Beer was not simply the prince of textual editors, he was also the king of indexers. He was a marvellous man, and lived what seemed to his friends to be the most satisfactory of intellectual and literary lives.

Award winners

The Wheatley Medal 'for an outstanding index published in the United Kingdom during the preceding year' ('The Wheatley Medal', 1970) was awarded by the Library Association and the Society of Indexers annually from 1961 to 2012 – but rarely to narrative indexes. As Piggott observed in 1991:

> Most of the medals had been awarded to compilers of bibliographies or to indexers of a long sequence of periodicals or of related documents either from an individual such as letters, or from a corporate body – its archives. (Piggott, 1991)

Matthews suggested an explanation for this (Matthews, personal communication, 1991):

> This kind of index receives very little attention from the Wheatley judges. [...] There seems to be a number of reasons, mainly to do with having to consider abstract rather than concrete matter, and trying to assess on the basis of value judgement rather than straight, clear fact. It must be so much easier to judge a legal, technological, scientific or medical work than a philosophical, literary or even biographical one.

Indeed, a publisher suggested that there should be separate awards for the Wheatley Medal: one for a book in the humanities, another for the sciences (Wace, 1975).

Besides, our biography indexes need their strings attached [see below, chapter 14], strings being generally prohibited, however, in the criteria for indexing awards (Lee, 2001; Weinberg, 1989).

The criteria used as guidelines by the Wheatley Medal selection committee published in 1974 (*The Indexer* 9(1), 22–3) included:

> 5. An index must have enough subheadings to avoid strings of undifferentiated location references.

Two years later, Geoffrey Hamilton reiterated (Hamilton, 1976):

> If there are numerous examples of strings with more than about

six undifferentiated references the index is almost certainly not going to achieve an outstanding grading.

As Jill Ford pointed out in 1993, 'The conditions and criteria during the 30-year span of the Medal's existence have changed', but they still included '[a]voidance of strings of undifferentiated references' (Ford, 1993).

In 2000 I sent an Open Letter to the Panel Judging the Wheatley Award which was printed in the newsletters of all the Societies of Indexers and in *Catalogue & Index*, complaining (Bell, 2000):

> The latest LA Reference Awards form still includes in the criteria for the Wheatley Medal 'for an outstanding printed index' the stipulation, 'Indexes will be judged on [...] avoidance of strings of undifferentiated page references'.

The following year the Chairman of the Wheatley Medal panel wrote (Lee, 2001):

> One of the things we are specifically asked to do is mark down if we see strings of undifferentiated page numbers [...] We have been criticized for criticizing strings, on the grounds that they sometimes must occur. A string of undifferentiated page numbers in itself is not a hangable crime, and I personally accept this, whilst generally not wanting to see too many of them.

The four narrative indexes described below managed to dodge this bullet.

(1) In 1962 the first Wheatley ever was awarded to *'Clemency' Canning* by Michael Maclagan (Macmillan, 1962), a centenary biography of Charles John, the 1st Earl Canning, Governor-General and the first Viceroy of India: a 35-page index to a 385-page book. The index was the work of the book's author, the first 'of any moment' that he had compiled. It was reviewed in *The Indexer* by G. Norman Knight (Knight, 1964), and later discussed by Mary Piggott as an example of an author's own index (Piggott, 1991). Maclagan was a British historian, antiquary and herald, Fellow and Tutor in Modern History at Trinity College, Oxford, for more than forty years, a long-serving officer of arms, and Lord Mayor of

Oxford 1970–1. Mary Piggott attributed his success as an indexer to his career:

> The index made by any author reflects the training he has had in his own discipline and also his own personality and experience of life. [Maclagan] thought chronologically, was scrupulously exact in presenting names and in distinguishing between separate instances of the same phenomenon [...] strove to fulfill the requirements of scholarship in accurate statement and citation [...] was also a man of affairs – he became Lord Mayor of Oxford in 1970 – and possibly that helped him to organize his procedure and announce it at some length at the beginning of his index. (Piggott, 1991)

(2) In 1967 the award was won by *Winston S. Churchill [...] vol. 2, Young statesman, 1901–1919* by Randolph S. Churchill (Heinemann, 1967); index by Knight. Richard Bancroft described the text of this proposed ten-volume series as:

> a historical work conceived on a huge scale. It covers nearly a hundred years and in this period nearly every figure and every issue of any political importance in Great Britain is treated, often in considerable detail. (Bancroft, 1968)

Knight, a civil servant who began freelance indexing in 1925 and instigated the founding of the Society of Indexers in 1957, serving as its first Chairman, had written in *The Indexer* the year before winning the Wheatley a full account of his preparation of the index to volume 1, often quoted in this book (Knight, 1966).

(3) The award for 1983 went to *The diary of Samuel Pepys. Vol. XI Index*, edited by Robert Latham and W. Matthews (Bell & Hyman, 1983); index by the first-mentioned editor. Reviews of this index appear or are quoted in *The Indexer* 13(4), 272–3 and 275, and 14(2), 138. Wellisch calls it 'an outstanding example of a modern narrative index that manages to provide the necessary context for every indexed item with a minimum of verbiage' (Wellisch, 1991). Robert Latham was successively Reader in History at Royal Holloway College, Professor of History at the

University of Toronto, a Fellow of Magdalene College, Cambridge, and Pepys Librarian until 1982, in charge of the collection of books, prints and manuscripts which Samuel Pepys left to his old college, as well as co-editor of this edition of Pepys' diary. Latham described the compilation of this index in two articles in *The Indexer* (Latham and Latham, 1980; Latham, 1984). The latter is accompanied by the reproduction of a page of it (from halfway through CAMBRIDGE to CARR, [WILLIAM]); while the preceding page, BUTLER to CAMBRIDGE, is reproduced in *The Indexer* **14**(3), 173. Its typography is further examined below, in Chapter 13.

(4) The Wheatley Medal for 1994 was awarded to Colin Matthew for the 862-page index to the 13 text volumes of *The Gladstone diaries* (Clarendon Press), which he also edited. This index exists both in print and as a database, capable of being searched in combinations not foreseen by the compiler and of being updated, expanded and corrected (Hird, 2000). Professor Matthew worked on the Gladstone diaries from 1970, compiling the index volume in 1994. He also wrote a two-volume life of Gladstone, and was editor of the *New dictionary of national biography*. He described the (team-)work of compiling the Gladstone diaries index in *The Indexer* **19**(4), Oct. 1995 257–64: 'Indexing Gladstone: from 5 x 3" cards to computer and database'.

In the US, the H. W. Wilson Company / American Society of Indexers Award for Excellence in Book Indexing, inaugurated in 1978, went for the first time in 1998 to the index to a book that could be described as at least part-soft: *Dead wrong: a death row lawyer speaks out against capital punishment* by Michael Mello (University of Wisconsin). The book, indexed by Laura Moss Gottlieb, was described by the Chair of the judging committee, Do Mi Stauber, as:

> a personal and passionate account of the author's experiences. As Mello says in the introduction, 'Story is the heart of the matter'. A book with this kind of narrative structure, which in this case includes a large amount of information about the legal system as well as being full of emotion, is extremely difficult to index and needs an unusual amount of analysis. Laura Gottlieb has gracefully extracted the conceptual material from this

narrative and made it accessible to the reader in a coherent index structure. [...] It's aimed at both a legal/professional and a general audience. [...] The wording of the subentries, especially, is elegant and descriptive, matching the tone of the text [...] the index is easy to read, even though it's full of so much information. (Stauber, 1998)

The book's indexer, Laura Gottlieb, described it as the author's

passionate account of his fourteen years as a lawyer trying to keep people living on Death Row from being killed by the state. It is an autobiographical narrative by a deeply feeling man, sensitive to the complexities of the human condition. He attempts to convince people to change the capital punishment system by moving them emotionally through storytelling. (Gottlieb, 1998)

Laura majored in philosophy and took further degrees in library science and English literature, worked as a librarian and editor, then took to indexing when at home with small children, 'without realizing that [she] had embarked on a career that would become addictive', and continued to work as a freelance indexer after returning part-time to librarianship (Bell, 2008b).

The ANZSI Medal for 2013 was awarded to Alan Walker's index to former Prime Minister John Howard's autobiography *Lazarus rising* (HarperCollins, 2011, revised edition). The convenor of the judging panel reported:

The indexer faced a considerable challenge in indexing this book because John Howard had a longer career than most politicians, and his career encompassed a number of portfolios both in opposition and in government. This meant the indexer was faced with organizing a tremendous mass of material and, most importantly, was required to use great discretion in giving appropriate weight to important, and less important, topics. The indexer also needed in-depth knowledge of Australian politics and history to do the work justice. Alan Walker met these challenges admirably, providing an extremely detailed and comprehensive index, which at the same time is clearly organized and easy to use.

The index is remarkable for an index to an autobiography in that there is no heading for the main protagonist, John Howard. It takes considerable courage for an indexer to make this decision, as often the entry for the protagonist in a biography or an autobiography is the most lengthy and detailed in the index. To not have an entry for the protagonist means that the indexer must make the information that would usually be found in that entry available by other means, namely subject indexing. The outstanding feature of this index is its subject analysis and the exhaustive subject headings which that analysis has generated. [...] An extensive network of cross-references anticipates readers' queries well. (Cousins, 2014)

In 2017 the Canadian ISC/SCI Ewart-Daveluy Award for Indexing Excellence was presented to Judy Dunlop for her indexing of *One child reading: my auto-bibliography* by Margaret Mackey (University of Alberta Press). The indexer had to combine the author's memories with theoretical discussion and textual analysis; the author commented that she was 'awestruck' by the 'sensitivity' of [the indexer's] reading (Awards roundup, 2017).

The following year, that award was presented to Audrey McClellan for her index to *Churchill and Fisher: Titans at the Admiralty* by Barry Gough (Seaforth Publishing).

The book focuses on the relationship between Winston Churchill, as first lord of the Admiralty, and John Fisher, as first sea lord of the British Navy [...] Audrey achieved a thorough and comprehensive coverage of all relevant topics and personal names, along with the interrelationships between and among topics and names, within the space constraints. (Awards roundup, 2018)

Audrey McClellan majored in English at the University of Victoria in British Columbia. Through the university's co-op programme she spent three terms at Harbour Publishing, editing books, writing indexes, and learning about book promotion and the publishing process. After graduation she worked in-house at Harbour Publishing, New Star Books, and International Self-Counsel Press before going freelance in 1997.

Since then she has worked as an editor and indexer of trade and academic books and textbooks.

Award-winning indexes to volumes of letters by five different correspondents are described in Chapter 1.

Cecelia Wittmann has compared subheadings used in award-winning and non-award-winning pairs of biographies, histories, and documentary texts – see Chapter 5.

Other good 'uns

Some other narrative indexes, lacking awards, have received high praise.

One has been commended by the Wheatley Panel: that to *Dickens* by Peter Ackroyd (Christopher Sinclair-Stevenson, 1990); a 41-page index to 1,083 pages of text. This was compiled by Douglas Matthews (who receives no acknowledgement in the volume as indexer). He comments, 'What was unusual about *Dickens* was its bulk, and the dominance of the central character', and that he was glad to have 'had some experience of the subject, having fairly recently compiled the index to vol. 6 of the Dickens letters (Clarendon Press, 1988). The consequent familiarity with Dickens and his circle was a great help' (Matthews, personal communication, 1991). This index was described by the Chair of the Wheatley Panel as 'lively, full of character, well organized, and as distinctive as the book it so ably complements' (Wheatley Medal, 1992). (In 1991 a paperback edition of this Dickens biography was published by Mandarin. The index appears to have been reset or run though a computer programme that unintelligently rearranged many of its subheadings; all comments made here on this index refer to the original, hardback edition which was the subject of the Wheatley Panel Commendation.)

Douglas Matthews, who has compiled so many of the indexes commended in this volume, and is its most-cited writer, compiled hundreds of indexes (his first in 1957) alongside his day job as Librarian of London Library. When the BBC mounted a radio programme in 1999 'in the form of a discussion between a biographer and an indexer,' Douglas was the selected representative of the second profession (Matthews, 1999). In the 2013 New Year's Honours List he was awarded an OBE, as 'Literary Indexer. For services to Literature'. Christopher Phipps, in a tribute to Douglas on his ninetieth birthday, wrote:

Douglas Matthews must easily win the competition for that most coveted of prizes for our lonely, long-distance profession: the named mention in the acknowledgements section. There he is often billed as 'prince among indexers'. [...] He is the epitome of what we must hope is not a dying breed, the scholarly librarian turned indexer [...] His indexes, so readily identifiable at first glance as 'a Douglas Matthews index', remain exemplars of concision, efficacy and wit. (Phipps, 2017)

Indeed, Douglas Matthews may be regarded as the proper successor to Esmond de Beer as 'king of indexers'.

In *Training in indexing* (M.I.T. Press, 1968) James Thornton cited his own selection of 'four masterly indexes, to which the student of indexing would do well to pin his faith [...] it is good practice to examine good indexes to learn the principles on which they were compiled' (Thornton, 1968). His choice included a biography, a diary and a collection of letters: respectively, the index to L. F. Powell's revision (1964) of Birkbeck Hill's edition of Boswell's *Life of Samuel Johnson* (Boswell, 1887); R. W. Chapman's to his edition of Samuel Johnson's letters, and E. S. de Beer's to his edition of John Evelyn's diary, all described above. Of the first, he added:

Had not Powell produced his own index, [I] would have included the one by his predecessor, Birkbeck Hill, an index produced in 1892 and one of the first major indexes that still satisfy the requirements of modern scholarship. Birkbeck Hill's contribution to the profession of indexing is his introduction of alphabetical order and categorization into the descriptive material or subheadings within each entry or article.

In her survey, 'Biography indexes reviewed' Catherine Sassen quoted the praise lavished on Joel Blanchard as editor and indexer of the *Mémoires* of Philippe De Commynes (Livre de poche, 2002) in a review (Sassen, 2012): 'Anyone wanting to locate a particular passage will be especially appreciative of Blanchard's index. Nearly two hundred pages in length, it provides detailed analytical coverage of all the mentions of persons, places and themes. The chapter index also provides a summary of the contents of each chapter.'

Narrative indexes sometimes appear in the 'Indexes praised' section of *The Indexer*'s regular feature, 'Indexes Reviewed'. These have received there the praise cited below (only one indexer named by the reviewer, alas):

- *War diaries 1939–1945*, by Field Marshal Lord Alanbrooke, ed. by Alex Danchev and Daniel Todman (Weidenfeld & Nicolson, 2001). 'The editors are to be congratulated on their work and on the excellent index, a model of its kind.' (Index by Douglas Matthews).

- *The double bond: Primo Levi: a biography* by Carole Angier (Farrar, Straus & Giroux, 2002). 'Scrupulously indexed'.

- *Somerset Maugham and the Maugham dynasty* by Bryan Connon (Sinclair Stevenson, 1997). 'Its index is superb'.

- *Michelangelo: a biography* by George Bull (Viking, 1995). 'The index [is] exhaustively detailed and efficient'.

- *Boris Yeltsin: a revolutionary life* by Leon Aron (HarperCollins, 2000). 'A comprehensive and painstakingly well-researched – and indexed – study'.

In 1998 Shirley Kessel, an American indexer, wrote to me: 'I've been looking at some indexes of biographies published in the UK. Two especially stand out. One is Roy Jenkins' biography of Gladstone; the other is the two-volume (soon to be three) biography of Keynes by Robert Skidelsky' (personal communication). *Gladstone* by Roy Jenkins (Macmillan, 1995; which volume won the Whitbread prize for that year) includes in Jenkins's preface an acknowledgement, 'Douglas Matthews, former librarian of the London Library, has once more compiled a complicated index'.

Skidelsky's *John Maynard Keynes, Vol. 1: Hopes Betrayed 1883–1920; Vol. 2: The Economist as Saviour, 1920–1937* was published by Macmillan, 1983 / 1992. Douglas Matthews indexed Vol. 2 (and is not listed in the three full pages of acknowledgements).

* * *

I feel that I should also expose some of my own attempts to implement the principles advocated herein, so list also some of my indexes to biographies:

Jane Austen by Claire Tomalin; Viking, 1998

Alistair Cooke by Nick Clarke; Weidenfeld & Nicolson, 1999

Emily Dickinson and the hill of science by Robin Peel; Fairleigh Dickinson University Press, 2009

Adam Ferguson: history, progress and human nature ed. E. Heath and V. Merolle; Pickering & Chatto, 2008

Thomas Hardy: the guarded life by Ralph Pite; Picador, 2006, 2008

Daughter of the desert by Georgina Howell; Pan Macmillan, 2006

Arthur Koestler: the homeless mind by David Cesarani; Heinemann, 1998

The world is what it is: the authorized biography of V.S. Naipaul by Patrick French; Picador, 2008

Rasputin: the last word by Edvard Radzinsky; Weidenfeld & Nicolson, 2000

Joshua Reynolds by Ian McIntyre; Allen Lane, 2003

Virginia Woolf: an inner life by Julia Briggs; Allen Lane, 2004

Articles about the **evaluation of indexes** that have appeared in *The Indexer* are:

Some requirements of good indexes. Richard Bancroft. **4**(1), 17–20

Criteria for awarding the Wheatley Medal. **6**(2), 63–6

What is a good index? F. H. C. Tatham. **8**(1), 23–8

The perfect index. John L. Thornton. **8**(4), 206–9

The inadequacies of book indexes: symposium. **9**(1), 1–9

Selective indexing: symposium. **9**(2), 59–65

How to recognize a good index. Geoffrey Hamilton. **10**(2), 49–53

Evaluating index systems: a review after Cranfield. John J. Regazzi. **12**(1), 14–21

Indexing biographies

The unconventional index and its merits. William S. Heckscher. **13**(1), 6–25

Assessing indexes. Jean Simpkins. **14**(3), 179–80

Index, how not to. John A. Vickers. **15**(3), 163–6

Sic, sic, sic! Jean Simpkins **16**(3), 104–5

Subheadings in award-winning book indexes: a quantitative evaluation. Cecelia Wittmann. **17**(1), 3–6

Authors as their own indexers. Mary Piggott. **17**(3), 161–6

Could still do better: the revised index to the Newman biography. John A. Vickers. **17**(3), 189–90

Unacademic indexing. John A. Vickers. **18**(1), 23–4

Oh, dear, what can the matter be *this* time? John A. Vickers **18**(3), 155–6

Information access or information anxiety? An exploratory evaluation of book index features. C. Jörgensen and E. D. Liddy. **20**(2), 64–8

Let's get usable! Susan C. Olason. **22**(2), 91–5

Judging indexes: the criteria for a good index. David Lee. **22**(4), 191–4

Do Mi's second rule or the functions of subheadings. Do Mi Stauber. **24**(4), 192–6

Biography indexes reviewed. Catherine Sassen. **30**(3), 136–9

The ANZSI Medal 2012: some thoughts on what makes a prize-winning index. ANZSI Medal Committee. **31**(1), 35–6

History indexes reviewed. Catherine Sassen. **31**(3), 105–9

Reflections on the Wilson judging for 2012. Margie Towery. **31**(3), C7

Evaluating an index together: Heartland chapter workshop. Laura A. Ewald. **31**(4), 168–9

ASI/EBSCO Publishing Award. **31**(4), 169–71

Evaluating indexes: observations on ANZSI experience. Sherrey Quinn **33**(3), 107–12

A full list of articles on this subject in *The Indexer* can be found on the website at https://www.theindexer.org/indexes/contents-by-category/ under Practice of indexing

3.   First read your book

Faced thus with little-known subject-matter, the indexer of life-stories should, ideally, read the text in hand straight through before starting to work on it – if only time permits!

Ideally, we should read the text to learn its subject matter, and come to know the material we are to work on, as a potter does his clay. We need to gain a perspective on the text, to know which will be major, which minor, subjects, which will recur and accrue large entries, needing careful management. We need *not* to be distracted from our work by sheer interest in the development of the text as we work through it, so read it first for inoculation! We must also avoid the risk of dismissing apparently negligible early mentions that may later prove to be significant first glimpses of important characters or themes. We must see the book not just item by item, to be reduced to minor, specific entries, but also the overall patterns of development to be allotted generalizing terms and chronological divisions. It is particularly difficult to index biographies at first sight.

Tom Murphy explored 'the possibilities of indexing as a teaching tool' for studying literature, as such indexing 'required a special kind of close reading – one that could not rest on merely superficial understandings but demanded a recursive flow, the constant back and forth of careful reading and re-reading' (Murphy, 2003).

To gain a clear, overall comprehension of the whole work, indexers really need to be supplied with all the parts of the volume that will help to give this full insight – those prelims, illustrations, chronologies, maps, notes, bibliographies and other appendages that are often withheld from us as 'they aren't yet available and they won't need to be indexed'. Included in the index, perhaps not – but included in and contributing to the indexer's understanding, they should be.

Preliminary reading also shows us the density of the text, so that, knowing the space allotted for the index and thus the allowable numbers of entries (remembering though that subheadings, expressed in words, take disproportionately more space than page references, expressed in figures), we can estimate the strike level of significance for which we allot entries, and the degree to which they can be broken down into subentries. Narrative indexing depends on and derives from close and sensitive reading of the entire text in hand. To enable this, it may be helpful for the publisher to send a copy of the text for advance reading by the indexer before the page proofs are available for indexing.

Laura Moss Gottlieb, who specializes in indexing academic books in the humanities, winner of the H. W. Wilson Company / American Society of Indexers Award for Excellence in Book Indexing in 1998, strongly advocates reading the whole book before setting finger to keyboard (Gottlieb, 1998).

> I believe that the job of every indexer is to be the author's most sympathetic reader: to understand what the author is saying and to provide a map to his or her views so that the reader can quickly and easily find them. [...] My primary indexing technique is simply this: *I read the whole book before I begin to index.* [...] The main point of reading the whole book is to follow and understand the author's argument before I get near the computer. This gives me the confidence that I understand the argument, know its main points, can locate related themes, and won't have to spend a lot of time going back through the page proofs trying desperately to locate material the importance of which I didn't realize until later. It feels like an ethical, confident way to index academic books of this type.

And Douglas Matthews insists:

> There can be no shortcutting that basic, dogged, analytical reading of the whole work and then arranging it to make the text easy for consultation, which is the essential function of the indexer. That is what takes the time, not the manner of recording the entries. (Matthews, 1996)

Analysis and annotation

Once we have seen the text steadily and whole, we may proceed to a second, entry-making reading. This is a more disjointed journey through the text, reducing it to its component parts and strands – *not* merely name- or capital-letter spotting! In deciding for which factors to make index entries, we are not extracting selected terms, leaving an unindexed mass, but reducing the entire text to denser units, with only the vaguest, most general passages not subsumed under some broad heading.

Indexers of biographies focus on one paragraph at a time to see what features in it, while keeping in mind the unit of the enveloping chapter and the relation of all its elements to the whole book – the *gestalt*. We are analysing and documenting human life and relationships at several levels – assuredly, a complex business. As Matthews puts it, discussing the narrative nature of biography:

> The index can be seen almost as an abstract of the life [...] but differs from the narrative in being able to signal any feature at any stage of a life. You might open a book at random and happen on something of interest; the index gives you a set of keys to particular and appropriate doors [...] A good index points out the main features in the landscape of a text. (Matthews, 1999)

As the biographical indexer works through a book, lists grow ever longer: the overall, single list that will form the ultimate index, and the subsidiary ones for each major character and theme, to be integrated eventually into the larger unit. As characters and topics recur after their first entry, a choice must be made for each further reference as to whether the new page number should merely be added to the others, inserted under one of the existing subheads, or under a new subheading. Lists of notes to be edited later into entries come to resemble jottings for an essay or article.

Many references are not closed at this point. 'JONES: seaside holiday 56–' may remain so, awaiting the closing page number perhaps until the final editing stage. Characters appear and disappear as on a stage – their entries and exits may be clearly apparent, but they remain on stage in the background, unmentioned, yet needing continuous watching, with perhaps an open-pagination reference maintained for them, and we must at some time establish the point where the reference should be terminated.

This read-through while making entries is disjointed in several ways. Not only is our manner of reading and working at this stage fragmented: read the text, mark it (with pen on page or highlighter on screen), key in entry, think, back to text; but also the indexer is consciously unravelling the carefully composed text, trying to understand the author's mind in order to undo their work of synthesis.

For each paragraph, several separate questions must be answered simultaneously. The simplest are, 'What is mentioned in this paragraph? Who (plural!) appear in it?' Then, for each character: 'What new things does the paragraph tell us about the characters and themes that have already appeared? Or, is this one merely continuing references we have already opened?' 'How are the contents of this paragraph contained within/related to the rest of the chapter/book?' The overall concepts, abstract themes, that pervade the book must also be watched – general events or developments in relationships, perhaps implied rather than stated, so that subheadings are needed for denoting OUTBREAK OF WAR; END OF AFFAIRE. *And meanwhile…*, we constantly have to note, *and meanwhile* […].

All the criteria of good indexes that seem most important to me – faithfully maintaining the attitudes of the text in the language used; correspondence of importance in the text with space allotted in the index; the most fitting arrangement of subheadings to form a coherent whole under each long entry – must derive from a close, sensitive reading of the text.

By the selection of items to specify subheadings, the indexer is choosing to emphasize particular aspects of the text over others – interpreting the text for the reader. Perhaps our hero, on a single page, on his thirtieth birthday, in 1949, in Surbiton, attends a socially important garden party, where he meets old friends, then falls and breaks his ankle. Which, or how many, aspects of this occasion/stage of his life would we pick out to designate in the subheadings? We have to determine the relative degrees of importance in the author's intention and the reader's response.

Coverage

Extraneous matter such as prologue, acknowledgements, illustrations, bibliography, and appendices may well qualify for inclusion in the indexes to biographies. I would take a specific decision as to what to include for each book, rather than advocating a general rule. I usually give an index reference to anyone in the acknowledgements who also appears in the text; I would not index the thanks to the author's wife for keeping the children quiet while he wrote, but would include reference to the widow of the book's hero who had made his papers available and answered questions about him; that is relevant to his life and relationships.

Illustrations should be included in the index if possible, even if we are indicating less their exact position in the volume than that there are in fact pictures of the people or places to be found. It can be difficult to get a list of the illustrations from the publisher in time to include them in the index, let alone the actual captions or the pictures themselves. If closer indexing of the pictures is not possible for these reasons, I include *ill.* at the end of the appropriate entries to convey that a search through the section of illustrations will be rewarded. Since photographs are usually gathered together in batches in the books, easily detectable from looking at the page edges, this does not seem quite inadequate information.

Hans Wellisch, though, advocated much closer indexing of illustrations in a biography, as well as of the bibliography:

> Pictures in a biography should not merely be indexed by a string of locators under the name of the biographee but also specified as to what they show about the person's life at various stages and in different environments or occupations. (Wellisch, 1991)

Wellisch also recommends either typographical differentiation of locators for illustrations by printing them in italics or boldface, adding an asterisk or enclosing them in square brackets, or 'the use of a subheading which makes it possible to specify not only the place but also the type of picture' (photo, portrait, sketches).

For maps, I will list the map title, but not its contents. Bibliographies, rather than being duplicated in the index, may best be covered by including their section or topic headings, if these have been supplied.

4. Naming names

Minor references to characters, or those making a single appearance in the book – ancestors, school friends in an early chapter, who then disappear from the life of the main character and the text – may appear simple to cope with. We list their names alone, without benefit of gloss or subhead (unless more than one character has the same name, when glosses should be provided – see below). Glosses may also be needed for names in the index when characters make their first appearances in the text unnamed, and need to be identified on the text page by the index user.

'Names-only indexing' sounds the simplest sort. There may, however, be many complexities in a name; causing much more than nominal difficulty for the indexer. The difficulties must be resolved, though. Douglas Matthews declares:

> I have always taken the view that so far as possible an index should be a self-sufficient reference tool, and in indexing historical works I am prepared to spend a great deal of time researching correct names and titles. (Matthews, 2004)

Alternative forms

People change their names. Women marry, maybe more than once, maybe reverting to a former name after divorce; writers adopt pseudonyms, actors stage names; criminals take aliases; people are ennobled, acquiring complexities of titles; they change names by deed poll for various motives (surely not just for spite against indexers). Knight reported, 'one lady who had been indexed under her married name actually reverted to her maiden name between one proof stage and the foundry pulls' (Knight, 1966). The only steadfast rule for indexing names can be that people should be findable – perhaps with the help of cross-references – under whichever possible version of their names they are likely to be sought, and identifiable when reached, as the person originally perhaps sought under another name, by confirmation in brackets (née, formerly, later, etc. with alternative versions).

Imposing rules of consistency, such as that *all* married women must be entered under their married name (or the first, or the last, of them), or *all* peers under their family name, may result in quite perversely obscure instances of the unfamiliar form being the chosen one (as well as according greater significance to status than to individuality). Particular principles adopted may be explained in preliminary notes, and a plethora of cross-references may point from any alternative callings to the selected one (*if* space allows – cross-references are space-devouring, usually taking at least two lines each).

Knight had to contend with peculiarity in the form of names of the family he was indexing:

> One problem [...] concerned the alphabetical arrangement of the Churchill family. It may not be universally known that Sir Winston himself had a hyphenated surname and the ever rightfully punctilious Court Circular right up to the end of 1951 invariably referred to him as Winston Spencer-Churchill. [...] But in a letter to his father as early as 1888 he explained: 'I never write myself Spencer Churchill but always Winston S. Churchill'. [...] Since scarcely anyone would dream of looking for his name or those of his parents, Lord and Lady Randolph, under 'S', they were indexed under 'C'. For the meticulous-minded, however, cross-referencing is provided in the entry under 'Spencer-Churchill'. (Knight, 1966)

Margaret Drabble also complained about hyphenated names in indexes, in her case from the user's point of view, with reference to writing her biography of Angus Wilson (Drabble, no date):

> Angus Wilson's family presented great problems of naming because they were Johnstone-Wilsons and it is not a good idea to write a biography of a hyphenated person because you have to look everything up twice over. If you don't find what you seek under one name you have to look it up under the other and this can double your research time.

A thoroughly punctilious index in the matter of name changes and alternatives is that to *Anthony Eden* by Robert Rhodes James (Weidenfeld & Nicolson, 1986. Only five years after the publication of that volume, I was quite unable to trace the name of the indexer: an indication of the small credit and accreditation that indexers receive). Quoted below is part of its preliminary note referring to treatment of names, followed by some of its main entries for these:

> Many people mentioned in the biography succeeded to titles or were created life peers after the events described; they are indexed either by surname or by their title at the time. Those who entered into their titles during the period covered will be found under their latest title, with the appropriate cross-reference(s) from their surname or previous title. To avoid overloading an already long index, the prefix 'Rt Hon' has been omitted throughout.

Brooke, Lady (Marjorie, *née* Eden, *later* Countess of Warwick) (sister)

Churchill, Clarissa (*later* Mrs Anthony Eden, *afterwards* Countess of Avon), *see* Eden, Clarissa

Dunglass, Lord (Alexander Douglas-Home, *later* 14th Earl of Home, q.v.)

Eden, Clarissa (*née* Churchill, *later* Mrs Anthony Eden, *afterwards* Lady Eden, *now* Countess of Avon)

Eden, John (Jack) (brother)

Eden, John Benedict (*now* Lord Eden of Winton) (nephew)

Evans, Sir Horace (*later* Baron Evans)

Home, 14th Earl of (Sir Alexander Douglas-Home, *later* Baron Home of the Hirsel): (as Lord Dunglass), PPS to AE (James, 1986)

Presumably, if space were short for the index, or the references few or casual, these names might not be so fully cited. Note here the variety of information given to supplement names: former and subsequent titles; nicknames; relationship to the central character of the book. Using the right name or title for people at the dates at which events being indexed occurred is considered above, in the section on indexing letters.

John Brown, meet John Brown

The opposite problem to a plethora of forms of name for one individual, of course, is name-sharing among several. John Vickers lamented:

> In the field with which I am best acquainted, not only is there a whole family of Wesleys (including at least three Samuels – father, son and grandson), but such potential hazards as a George Whitefield (1714–1770) and a totally unrelated near-namesake, George Whitfield (1753–1832), whose surnames are sometimes spelled interchangeably. Similarly, English literature has *two* Samuel Butlers (died 1680 and 1912 respectively); while Samuel Johnson the author of the hymn 'City of God, how broad and far' is *not* the Samuel Johnson of 18th-century Grub Street. (Vickers, 1991)

Where more than one character has the same name, some gloss should be given to each to differentiate them: their dates if known; their relationship if any (Sr, Jr; son of above); profession; role in the book; or whatever information is available to cite.

Philip Marris, producing a family history stretching back 30 generations, replete with myriad Georges, Johns, Thomasses, and Williams of the same ilk, distinguished them by allotting each individual their own generation number in parentheses, from de Marč, Osbert / Otbert (1), a Domesday tenant whose son fought at the Battle of Hastings in 1066, to Marris, Richard Quentery (30), who served in the RAF in World War II (Marris, 2019).

Who are all these people?

There may, too, be those incompletely named in our books. We should try to ensure that all are named in full in the index. Surnames alone in an index are not satisfactory – we should try to provide forenames or initials if the text does not supply them, by consulting appropriate reference books or googling for public figures, or asking the author for forenames of the otherwise unknown. Names must be expanded and identities hunted down. 'Jones, Mr', clearly needs expansion or explanation; and alphabetical order will be affected by having eight Joneses with forenames listed, with nameless 'Mr', or – , or (gardener). Readers who know that his name was in fact William may miss him, initial-less at the top of the list.

Where full names are not available, epithets may be provided as glosses:

Annie (housemaid)
Edward (birthday party guest)
Jones, Mr (tailor)

For several members of the same family, with the same surname, it is best to specify in brackets their relationship to the main character. This breaks up long columns of the same name with helpful information, especially when a relative – the mother, perhaps – is being sought without the forename being known. The names of the families of the subjects of biographies are quite likely not to be widely known.

Glosses explain the main entry, and are enclosed in brackets, as distinct from subheadings, which specify particular references subdivided under the main entry.

Knight praised the glosses used in the *'Clemency' Canning* index (Knight, 1964):

Of the many unusual excellences in this index I must mention just one. Where the name of a historical character occurs as a main heading, in nearly every case it is followed by the date of death in brackets. This innovation, which is particularly useful in a historical biography, must have involved considerable research [how lucky we are today to have the Internet!]. Where he has been unable to supply the date of death the indexer sometimes replaces it with a brief but colourful description, as in the following: Khanlar Mirza, craven Persian prince, 53.

Knight was generous indeed with his own glosses for the Churchill series (Knight, 1966):

As regards my entries generally, these will be found to be somewhat fuller than is common in today's practice. That is to say, I was not content with providing a mere list of proper names and subjects, but in nearly every case supplied either a brief description of the item forming the heading or else briefly what happened to him, her, or it, in the text.

This information included dates and other details often 'not available in the text, and involved a good deal of research'. Knight describes one example:

> When he was at his preparatory school, Winston twice wrote to his mother expressing a desire to see Buffalo Bill. I felt that the mere heading: Buffalo Bill, 90 *bis* rather lacked point. Accordingly my entry runs: Buffalo Bill (W.F. Cody, 1845–1917), WSC wants to see (1887), 90 *bis*

The preface to the volume stated, 'the necessary details of rank and identification will be found in the index'. Knight particularly considers the question of giving dates after names in the index:

> I think that in historical works particularly, the practice is a useful one, although of course it involves more work for the indexer.

(Again, our sympathies go to the pre-Internet indexer!)

De Beer tells us, 'For persons Dr Powell [in the index to Boswell's *Life of Johnson*] inserts dates of birth and death and a biographical definition: e.g. Abington, Mrs Frances, 1737–1815, actress. He comments, 'This is requisite where it identifies or distinguishes persons, but elsewhere seems to me intrusive' (de Beer, 1967).

Errors and inconsistencies

We must also check that the spelling of names is correct. Sir Alec Guinness or Guiness? We are not necessarily querying the author's accuracy; typesetting errors in the proofs may be faithfully copied in the index. Indexers, as they collocate references, are likely to discover inconsistencies and omissions in the text that have escaped notice throughout the production process until this stage. Only the indexer is likely to realize that a character appears as Ann or Miss Phillips on page 26, Anne or Philips on 126, or to ask for certain missing forenames to complete name entries – thus drawing attention to the fact that the full names should really have been given to start with – and requesting a pronouncement on the correct spellings for the index. This may have a knock-on effect: Philipps or Phillips may have to be moved in alphabetical sequence, and Jones, Mr, sink from the top of the Jones column to the bottom as Jones, William.

Matthews claims that indexers do more than compile the index, functioning also as 'longstop copy editors', or 'test drivers', finding unnoticed errors and inconsistencies in the text in time to alert the author (Matthews, 1993).

Lord, My

The complications of indexing the peerage are horrendous. Clear, detailed guidance is offered by David Lee, on the degrees of British peerage, the particular problems of Ladies' names, hyphenation, and form and choice of name for indexes (Lee, 1991). He advocates that peers should be indexed by the name by which they are best known, rather than according to any rigidly standardized principle, with cross-references from alternative forms (if space permits), except that:

> If there are many members of a family dealt with in the book [...] some with titles, others with courtesy titles and others with surnames and forenames alone, the temptation to standardize on the use of the patronymic only (and refer from titles) [...] probably should not be resisted.

Maclagan states in the note at the head of the index to *'Clemency' Canning* (Knight, 1964):

> Historical personages are given under the name by which they are best known, e.g., Palmerston, not Temple, but Vernon Smith, not Lord Lyveden.

Pseudonyms

Pseudonyms and nicknames can cause problems beyond a profusion of cross-referencing if alternative versions are used through long sequences of the text. In *Stalin* (Hodder & Stoughton, 1995) through the section describing his childhood, he was referred to as 'Soso', his nickname then; later by his code-name of 'Koba'. Readers searching for references to him at those periods might not recognize these pseudonyms as denoting the later so-called 'Stalin'. My entry for him in the index read:

> Stalin (Joseph V. Dzhugashvili; childhood name 'Soso'; later
> pseudonym 'Koba')

A further complication with pseudonyms such as Stalin is that they stand alone, with no forenames; but have become so commonly known that the real-life forenames are often, incorrectly, attached to them – as, Stalin, Joseph. Other examples should correctly appear as:

> Molière (Jean-Baptiste Poquelin)
> Stendhal (Henri-Marie Beyle)

Articles on **indexing names** that have appeared in *The Indexer* are:

Arrangement of entries in Post Office telephone directories. Inland Telecommunications Department **2**(4), 142–3

The hereditary peerage. Hebe Jerrold. **3**(3), 130

Indexing peers. M. D. Anderson. **4**(2), 51

Post Office filing. M. Gorman & G. N. Knight. **7**(3), 118–20

Developing a system of indexing surnames in the Home Office. John L. Rush. **12**(2), 81–2

Name of an author! Anne B. Piternick **18**(2), 95–9

Coping with a title: the indexer and the British aristocracy. David Lee **17**(3), 155–60

Cataloging rules and tools: an aid for the indexing of names. Debra Spidal. **30**(4), 186–90

Personal names in indexes. Susan Curran. **36**(3), 108–14

See also *Indexing names*. Noeline Bridge (ed). Medford, NJ: Information Today Inc., 2012.

For advice on what to do about variant spellings of what is clearly the same surname in the period before spelling was standardized, how to deal with patronymics and aliases, surname prefixes – English and foreign, medieval and modern see R. F. Hunnisett, *Indexing for editors*. London: British Records Association, 1997.

Foreign names may cause particular problems to the indexer. For a full list of articles that have appeared in *The Indexer* on countries and languages, see 'Countries and languages' in 'Contents by category' on *The Indexer*'s website.

5. Coming to terms: subheadings

The official criteria for the language to be used for indexing militate against soft-text indexers. Soft texts may be the individual products of imaginative writers with particular vision, expressed in sensitive, subtle language that contains and deploys much more than mere information. Soft indexers must employ a flexible range of vocabulary to meet the authors' individual perception and expression. The words we choose to use in our indexes – besides the predetermined nouns – involve several different principles and difficulties, and must meet several criteria. This may be found an enjoyable challenge and skill: Robert Latham spoke of the pleasures of indexing as partly 'those of a Victorian paper game [...] you have to find the appropriate word or words to summarize or "indicate" the subject of the reference or references' (Latham, 1984).

The terms to be used in main headings – most usually nouns – indexers can pick directly from the text, as enjoined by BS ISO 999 clause 7.2.1.2: 'Headings should be chosen from the terminology employed in the document', perhaps enhanced by glosses as considered above (Chapter 4). The subheadings, though, must often be of our own devising, to convey the tenor of the text indicated. They may be generalizing terms not used in the text: CHARACTER, CHILDHOOD, CAREER, HEALTH, SOCIAL LIFE; or they may be supplied by us as précis of the passages. Cecelia Wittmann found:

> Only 20% of the subheadings in indexes to historical narratives closely match the text, probably because the task for the indexer here is principally to summarize the various events and ideas described in the text, not to provide access to the author's own words. (Wittmann, 1990)

Cleveland and Cleveland (1983) distinguish between *assigned-term indexing language*, where the indexer must 'assign terms or descriptors on the basis of subjective interpretation of the concepts implied in the document', and *derived-term systems*, or *indexing by extraction*, in which the indexer (or computer) 'selects the terms to be used directly from the text being indexed'. The former type involves 'more intellectual effort'.

In devising our subheadings, we bring to bear all the skills learned in English lessons for précis or summary: analysing the text; identifying the central, most important topics of each passage; and devising the most concise and appropriate terms in which to encapsulate the ideas. Carey declared the compilation of subheadings 'the task that calls for the indexer's highest skill of all' (Carey, 1961).

Christopher Phipps (2102) claims 'in our formation of headings [...] we should in a small way allow ourselves something of the flair and enjoyment of creative writing' and quotes the historian Hugh Trevor-Roper as saying, 'the index must be readable in itself, continuously, as an added chapter'.

An example of such an indexer-created, splendidly suitable to the text, subheading comes at the end of Phipps's section in his index to *Samuel Johnson: A Biography* by Peter Martin (Weidenfeld & Nicolson, 2008) about Johnson's labours on the construction of his *Dictionary*:

> Robert Dodsley's idea for a dictionary; planning the *Dictionary*; work begins; and comes to a screeching halt

Douglas Matthews gives another example of such interpretative indexing, in his index to Laurence Olivier's autobiography, *Confessions of an actor* (Weidenfeld & Nicholson, 1982). This includes Olivier's account of how he met Vivien Leigh, fell in love with her, and conducted a furtive affair with her for two years while he was still married to his first wife, Jill Esmond. Esmond herself makes no appearance through these pages of the text. But her entry in the index cannot omit reference to the affair; it impinged so greatly on her. The penultimate subheading in the index entry that Douglas contrived for *Esmond, Jill*, is

> – supplanted by Vivien Leigh

That term does not appear in Oliver's writing. It derives purely from Matthews' analysis and interpretation of the text.

Qualities to aim for

Wittmann compared subheadings used in award-winning and non-award-winning pairs of biographies, histories, and documentary texts (including the biographies of Canning and Churchill cited above) (Wittmann, 1990). She drew conclusions about the differences between award-winning and ordinary indexes, and between narrative and documentary indexes. Among her findings were:

> Subheadings in award-winning indexes are more consistently content-rich than the subheadings in other indexes.

> Subheadings in award-winning indexes are vivid and concise, conveying in a few words the essence of the material indexed; in contrast, the subheadings in other indexes are often cryptic, rambling, or vague.

> Subheadings in indexes to historical narratives average about five words in length [compared to subheadings half as long in indexes to texts consisting principally of documents] [...] probably because they are phrases summarizing an event described in the text.

> An overwhelming majority of the subheadings in award-winning indexes began with such significant words as nouns, verbs or participles.

> In all the award-winning indexes, topical subheadings predominate; that is, the subheadings are not syntactically related to the main heading under which they occur. (E.g.: Bengal army / enlistment terms (topical subheading)

And the subheadings are direct-order, the heading and subheading together forming a natural phrase, such as:

> NORWEGIANS / take British wives

Non-award-winning indexes, by contrast, have chiefly indirect-order subheadings, which have to be read inverted, moving the subheading before the main heading, to form a phrase, as:

NOVAYA ZEMLYA / latitude of

These, then, are the characteristics to aim for in the subheadings we provide to narrative texts: vivid, content-rich, topical rather than syntactical, concise, about five words long, beginning with a significant word, and forming a natural phrase in direct order.

We must also bear in mind just what degree of specification is needed in our subheadings – what possible question of the reader's we are answering. This may be either, 'Where can I find the information I know is in this book?' when the reader already knows what is there to be found, and seeks only identification of the items in the index; or, 'What does this book tell me about the person?' This one is more difficult to answer, and our choice of terms here must be highly informative.

Yet there can be no accepted *correct* version of subheadings for a given biography. Let us compare two different entries for the same narrative thread in one (auto)biography – that of Samuel Pepys. This text is told in the first person; the indexer has to interpret Pepys's own version of events for third parties. In the first example, the index to H. B. Wheatley's nine-volume edition of Pepys diary, of 1914, we find:

> Willet (Deb), Mrs. Pepys's new girl, arrives; taken to Brampton; Mrs Pepys is jealous of her; Pepys kisses her; combs Pepys's hair; her birthplace at Bristol; Mrs. Pepys catches Samuel embracing her; Pepys discharges her, and advises her never to see him again; her aunt.
> Then, {alluded to} [ten lines of page numbers].

Seventy years later, the Wheatley award for 1983 went to Robert Latham for his index to his 11-volume edition of the diary. He gave WILLET, Deb, companion to EP (Elizabeth Pepys) a fuller, franker treatment divided into four paragraphs – APPEARANCE: AS EP'S COMPANION: P'S AFFAIR WITH: and SOCIAL. Under P'S AFFAIR WITH in Latham's index come –

> P pleased with; EP jealous; P kisses; caresses; discovered by EP; her rage and P's guilt; P fears she must leave; is prevented from seeing; her confession; and dismissal; P searches for; EP threatens to slit her nose; P never to see again; [...] sees in street; EP makes jealous scenes; threatens him with hot

> tongs; he meets by chance; [...] winks at P in street; moves to Greenwich [...]

Those are two quite different index entries for exactly the same text. But we cannot suggest that either is *wrong*: the first is endorsed by 'the father of indexing', Wheatley himself, as the volume editor; the second won the award bestowed in Wheatley's name! The devising of subheadings for biographies is a subjective, not standardized, matter.

Language fit for literature

ISO, 1996 encourages the omission of prepositions in subheadings. This may result in indexes that rap out basic elements of information in staccato fashion, suitable for scanning and consultation rather than reading. The absence of prepositions produces a vague suggestion of connection, 'related in some way to'. The language of the indexes for narratives should rather flow in natural reading fashion; we are not attempting to boil down the text and extract basic information items, but to mirror it in miniature and guide readers through a condensed world of characters and ideas. In soft indexing, there is much virtue in prepositions.

The language used should complement that of the text. Latham 'hoped to capture in the index the flavour of the diary', and attributed much of his success in indexing Pepys to the help of his wife with her expertise in word games, as they sought 'the appropriate word for comprehensive headings or verbal formulas for a whole series of related subjects' (Latham and Latham, 1980). Part of de Beer's praise for Powell's index was that it 'reflects the conversable character of the book to which it is attached' (de Beer, 1967). Bancroft writes of Knight's index to Churchill, 'the choice of wording for the entries gives the sense of the item referred to fairly and fully', and was described as 'precept put into practice with elegance and precision' (Bancroft, 1968). The Wilson Panel's praise of Gottlieb's index to *Dead wrong* included, 'the wording of the sub-entries, especially, is elegant and descriptive, matching the tone of the text' (Stauber, 1998) – while Gottlieb herself wrote of Margie Towery's award-winning index to *The letters of Matthew Arnold*, 'The language is lovely' (M. Anderson, 2002).

Bancroft urges consistency of style in subheadings: 'In some indexes the use of the author's words is very effective but they must not be mixed indiscriminately with the indexer's own rephrasing' (Bancroft, 1964). Wellisch writes: 'Good narrative indexing provides an opportunity for the indexer to be creative in paraphrasing the text, using concise and terse formulations taking up a minimum of space yet conveying the necessary context for the benefit of users (1991).

And ...

The use of AND in subheadings to indicate unspecified relationship or dealings is often deplored as overly vague. However, to abstain from specification is to avoid *excluding* any aspect of the relationship, and this may be what we intend; *all* aspects may be relevant to the context, meet to be indicated; then a delimiter is not wanted: specific selection may entail an incongruous reduction of significance. In indexes to human lives, AND usually stands for general RELATIONS WITH or DEALINGS WITH; certainly it is a neater phrase than either, as well as usefully open-ended, allowing a totality of possibilities.

Douglas Matthews writes of AND, 'It has the virtue of blandness, making only a simple association and passing no judgments' (Matthews, personal communication, 1991). It thus solves the problem of bias: 'and' has a valuable neutrality compared to 'hostile feelings towards', 'guilty intentions towards'. The preliminary note to James Thornton's indexes to the letters of Charles Dickens includes: 'the word "and" is sometimes used to mean "in relation to" or where the connection would otherwise require a lengthy explanation' (Knight, 1970).

Articles on *language for indexing* that have appeared in *The Indexer* are:

Syntactic and semantic relationships – or: a review of PRECIS.
  P. F. Broxis. **10**(1), 54–9
Linguistics and indexing. David Crystal. **14**(1), 3–7
Indexing a reference grammar. David Crystal. **15**(2), 67–72
Natural-language processing and automatic indexing. C. Korycinski &
  A. F. Newell. **17**(1), 21–9

Indexing biographies

Natural-language processing and automatic indexing: a reply. Kevin
    P. Jones. **17**(2), 114–15
Bias in indexing and loaded language. Hazel K. Bell. **17**(3), 173–7
Selected linguistic problems in indexing within the Canadian context.
    Lisa Rasmussen. **18**(2), 87–91

For foreign languages, see 'Countries and languages' in 'Contents by
category' on *The Indexer*'s website.

Articles on **aspect/topic ('aboutness')** that have appeared in *The Indexer* are:

Why indexing fails the researcher. Bella Hass Weinberg. **16**(1), 3–6
Academic indexing: what's it all about? Ross J. Todd. **18**(2), 101–4
Subject analysis and indexing. Hanne Albrechtsen. **18**(4), 219–24
Is there anybody there? David Crystal. **19**(3), 153–4
All in the mind: concept analysis in indexing. John Farrow. **19**(4),
    243–4
Reverse indexing. David Crystal. **26**(1), 14–17
On aboutness. Kate Mertes. **35**(2), 77–8

6. The perils of partiality

Don't show your feelings

There is also the question of attitude implied by the language we use. Choice of terms is a great give-away, as in the famous conjugation, 'I practise fine economy / you are somewhat parsimonious / he is a right old skinflint'. Recording/presenting/interpreting implies the recorder's view of the event; and indexers must ensure that the attitudes implied in the index accord with those of the text.

A feminist dictionary (Kramerae, 1985) proclaims the power of the indexer to impose their views:

> Even the indexing of a book may constitute a subversive feminist action. An index entry in the 1976 edition of *Williams' Obstetrics*, a medical 'bible' edited by Jack A. Pritchard and Paul C. MacDonald, reads CHAUVINISM, MALE, variable amounts, 1–923; the 1980 edition reads CHAUVINISM, MALE, voluminous amounts, 1–1102. The preface thanks Signe Pritchard for her indexing skills.

Piggott quotes from Maclagan's index to *'Clemency' Canning*, observing, 'There is an individuality about some of his entries that would be foreign to an outsider's' (Piggott, 1991):

> Hewitt, General: obese and inactive at Meerut
> Indian Mutiny: stamping out last embers
> Telegram, New Yankee word for 'telegraphic despatch'
> Heralds, College of, 'slowest moving body known'

These are fine examples of deliberate reinforcement in the index of the attitudes expressed by the author in the text (the author in this case being the indexer). This must not be overdone, however: an index is not the proper place for promoting political hostility or partisanship, as illustrated by the following examples from the opposite extremes of approval and disapproval.

For sheer, over-the-top attack, look at a few of the 140 subheadings under Reagan, Ronald Wilson in *The clothes have no emperor: a chronicle of the Reagan years* (by Paul Slanksy; Fireside Books, 1989):

> blames Carter; blames Congress; blames the media; blames miscellaneous others; cancerous pimple called 'friend' by; confusion admitted by; detachment from reality imputed to; disbelief by public of; gloating by enemies of; inability to answer questions of; macho bluster of; mistakes admitted and not admitted by; [...]

More recently, here are some subheadings appearing under TRUMP, DONALD in the index to *This fight is our fight: The Battle to Save America's Middle Class* by E. Warren (Collins, 2017):

> bait-and-switch; bigotry and; corporate influences on; 'nasty woman' comment of; tax returns and; trickle-down and; tweetstorms vs.

On the other hand, the autobiography of Joseph Bonanno, a Sicilian Mafia leader (*A man of honour*, Deutsch, 1983), includes under his own entry in the index:

> generosity of; handsomeness of; intellect of; language skills of; tact of; wit of

Testing for validity – following some of these encomia to the only text indicated, we find that 'handsomeness of, 175' leads only to 'In general, people considered me an attractive man'; 'intellect of, 176', to, 'They kindly praised my charm and intelligence'; and 'wit of, 168' to, 'They used to say that I was the toasting champion of the inner table' – for which no example is vouchsafed.

Opposing attitudes conveyed by the wording of subheadings in the same index are nicely shown by a contrasting pair in Elizabeth Longford's biography, *Byron* (Hutchinson / Weidenfeld & Nicolson, 1976):

> Byron, George Gordon, 6th Lord: [...] his courtship and marriage, 60–79

Byron, Annabella, *née* Milbanke, wife of B. [...] vicissitudes of her marriage, 71–7

The term 'vicissitudes' does not occur in the text.

It is not only the opinions of the author, as expressed in the text, that may be trumpeted loud in the index. Philip Hensher (2004) warns indexers against indulging their own partialities: 'The potential for revenge and mockery in indexing is very high.' Indeed. An outstanding example must be the index to *A slight and delicate creature*, the memoirs of Margaret Cook (Weidenfeld & Nicolson, 1999), surely compiled by the author, the publicly deserted wife of British Foreign Secretary Robin Cook. His entry includes the subheadings: OUTBURSTS OF TEMPER; AND GUILT TRANSFERENCE; HEAVY DRINKING; WEIGHT PROBLEMS; SEXUAL DIFFICULTIES. And indexing power seems to have gone to the head of the indexer of *My trade: a short history of British journalism* by Andrew Marr (Pan, 2005). It contains the unsolicited entry:

Fallon, Ivan, triumphant and brave journalistic career of, unaccountably not mentioned.

Matthews, though, records suppressing his own reaction to the text he was indexing in his 'most unpleasant commission, an English version of Hitler's *Mein Kampf*':

This task almost forced me to abandon professional objectivity, but I gritted my teeth, suppressed my prejudices, and hope that I succeeded in turning in an accurate and disinterested product. (Matthews, 1993)

He wrote there of this need for impartiality:

It was tempting to slant the entries, for example, to make a subheading 'poisonous hatred of Jews'; but that would be inappropriate, while the neutral 'anti-Semitism' is exact and, I think, more effective because it is cooler. The text should say it all; the index merely directs the reader to where to look.

Putting it nicely

I once indexed a book by a hotel proprietor, presented as his diary, apparently genuinely so. I will not name the book or the author.

The text ran through a year of life in the hotel, using real names. The staff made frequent – almost daily – insignificant appearances, hovering perpetually in the background. They could not be omitted from the index, looming large in the text as a whole; but almost none of their references merited the distinction of subheadings, so that blocks of undifferentiated, unavoidable page numbers appeared after those names.

Two staff members, though, were each also accorded some long page-runs that could well have been separated out from the many insignificant references and distinguished by subheadings. However, both passages were, I thought, most intemperately written, suffused with the diarist/employer's unrestrained resentment and disapproval.

One named staff member was reported to be in the throes of a clandestine and passionate affair with [real name given – another staff member]. A lengthy passage about the second caused me to draw the attention of the publisher to it with a view to possible libel. The text presented the employee as guilty of under-charging his visiting prospective employer by £55, then of gross misconduct. Later he was referred to as the unscrupulous rat [real name].

Accurate subheadings for these passages would be 'adulterous affair', 'decline in performance' and 'dismissed'. But the book is written with such strong subjective bias, vigorously expressing the author's hostile opinions, that I wondered whether such authors' attitudes should be reflected/reinforced in an index, or whether indexers should not rather strive for neutral terms, avoiding value judgements, even when the text makes its prejudices all too apparent? Moreover, to allot subheadings for those passages only in the long and otherwise blameless entries for those two characters would have made them unwarrantably conspicuous.

If I had chosen to modify those index entries, substituting 'extra-marital affair' and 'last days at [named hotel]', these terms, far from matching the tone of the text, would have distorted it, euphemistically. Should indexers indulge in euphemism any more than in hostile bias, which we know to be out of order?

Linguistic limitation

Some difficulties in devising subheadings arise from the insufficient terms available to describe human life and its relationships in all their variety and shades, particularly as our language evolves more slowly than society changes. A number of terms I have felt the need of in indexing lives are simply lacking. What, for instance, do we call the period between meeting and becoming engaged, or co-habiting – often needed in breaking up main entries into chronological stages? COURTSHIP would once have met the case – but what now?

What-d'you-call-her?

Social problems abound today as parents wonder how to introduce or refer to the non-married life and love partners of their children – a missing term ever more required in modern biographies, especially for glosses. It was so easy to insert a formal (wife of …) or to provide subheadings, (marries …), (marriage), (marital relations). When the ceremonies have been omitted, what terms may we use? A jovial, 'This is my non-daughter-in-law' may do at social occasions, but 'non-wife' is not a suitable term for a printed index. Ours not to censure or condemn, but (mistress of), (seduces/succumbs to), may appear the only terms available. 'Partner' is pre-empted, already denoting a strictly business relationship, and its use in an amorous context may lead to embarrassing confusion.

Penelope Lively expressed the difficulty in her novel, *Cleopatra's sister* (Viking, 1993):

> Vivien referred to him as her partner, an expression Howard detested. He never found any satisfactory term for her: girlfriend seemed derogatory for a woman in her late thirties. He was reduced to the circumlocution of 'the person I share a flat with', which contained an ambiguity about sexual orientation, but woman, in this context, sounded faintly patronizing.

Correspondence in *The Times* in 1992 following an article entitled 'A person's most significant decision' suggested 'concubine', 'constant and ever-loving companion', 'current attachment', 'stablemate', 'bidie-in'

(Scottish), 'possleque' (person of opposite sex sharing living quarters), 'consort', 'sleeping partner' and 'co-vivant' (Diamond, 1992). Indexers, take your pick.

When women to be included in the index are referred to by their forenames only, we must either ask the author for the surnames – these having perhaps been deliberately withheld from the text, tactfully, so unlikely to be divulged for identification in the index; or, if we index them just as Jane, Susan, N or M, we need explanatory glosses – what? We must find non-censorious terms to indicate various passionate relationships outside marriage – not easy.

Illegitimate is another accurate, sometimes necessary term which regrettably smacks of disapproval. Relationships portrayed in the text may be warm and accepting, but our concise index terminology introduces censorious overtones through the connotations of the language available. We cannot maintain apparent neutrality in the absence of non-evaluative language. Authors can be subtle and discreet in their writing, with implication only; indexers have to condense their meanings to blunt labels.

Specific groups claim the right to self-identification by names of their own choice to replace those long accorded them. People with disabilities is sought to replace disabled, the. In indexes, we need the terms that are the most concise and the most likely to be sought by general readers, rather than lengthier, desired ones: different criteria from those of the author, and, maybe, from those of the subjects of the text.

In political contexts the choice of term may imply judging between alternative principles or policies. We must choose to use assassination, execution or murder; joins terrorists or freedom fighters; in crowd or mob; sees street protest or riot; helps refugees or illegal immigrants. Possible choices of term betray allegiance and allot approval or condemnation: our language is not value-free.

Feminists decry our language as patriarchal, male-dominated, alienating women, and denying them freedom of discourse, echoing Thomas Hardy's Bathsheba who declared: 'It is difficult for a woman to define her feelings in a language which is chiefly made by men to express theirs' (Hardy, 1874). Dale Spender, who challenged conventional perceptions of the way we use words in her *Man made language*

(Thorsons, 1985), turned her attention to man-made indexes when she undertook the indexing of her own *Women of ideas: and what men have done to them* (Pandora Press, 1988). She wrote to her sister.

> It was one thing to recognise that conventional indexes make women's experience and priorities invisible, but quite another to work out a new conceptualisation. [...] I think up ways of naming from women's perspective [...] We have put in the entry 'loving husbands' and along with it 'Radical men' and then have listed Bertrand Russell and John Stuart Mill for example, and have also cross-referenced them with 'champions of women's rights'. [...] By far the biggest entry is 'Harassment' – there must be a reference on every page [...] it is a practical way of saying that we don't have to accept the classification system that men have devised. (Spender, 1986)

Most certainly this index would successfully promulgate the attitudes of the author – but it hardly seems to promise an efficient finding aid, as she concludes her letter:

> I have deliberately refrained from indexing any men who are mentioned in the text on the grounds that what is good for the gander is good for the goose [...] how many indexes in books written by men make women invisible?

The book's 800 pages include a general index and an index of names, each seven pages long. The first is provided with a 16-line polemical headnote, and duly includes the headings:

> abuse of women; angry women see disagreeable women; appropriation of women's resources; burial of women's contributions; chivalry, non-existent nature of; contempt for women; economics, female (sexual economics).

The heading, harassment, indeed has a solid 21 lines of page-references: a whole ball of string.

The constraint of standardization

Another constraint on our terminology and expression may result from the use of thesauri and 'predetermined lists of subdivisions in subject catalogues', which, Bella Hass Weinberg points out, 'do not permit exact specification of the aspect or point-of-view of the topic' (Weinberg, 1988). How much more clumsy to impose standard terms on individual experience!

Weinberg distinguished between indexes focusing on aboutness, or topic – merely specifying the subject of the reference – and aspect, or comment – reporting the actual comment of the reference, defined by John Lyons as 'that part of the utterance which adds something new and thus communicates information' (Lyons, 1968). For narrative indexes, concerned with human lives which are not standardized nor lived according to predetermined terms and sub-terms, full aspect headings are necessary to convey the individual content, and resorting to thesauri other than those of vocabulary alone may prove inapplicable or falsifying. Assignation to predetermined headings may mean distorting our entries to fit within the general pattern, rather than emphasizing their individual content; cramming concepts into ill-fitting hand-me-down coatings rather than providing them with proper made-to-measure suits.

Standardization is opposed to subtlety and differentiation. The repeated use of the same subheading to cover several passages of the text may clumsily mask a subtle variation in apparently similar passages.

Ultimately it is the Whorfian hypothesis, that language determines thought, that governs our terminology in indexing (Whorf, 1956). His essay is prefaced by a quotation from Edward Sapir:

> Human beings do not live in the objective world alone, nor alone in the world of social activity as ordinarily understood, but are very much at the mercy of the particular language which has become the medium of expression for that society.

The preface to *Animal liberation* makes the same point regarding linguistic bias (Singer, 1977):

> The English language, like other languages, reflects the prejudices of its users. So authors who wish to challenge these prejudices

are in a well-known type of bind: either they use language that reinforces the very prejudices they wish to challenge, or else they fail to communicate with their audience.

'Have you stopped beating your wife ...?'
Linguistic limitation can best be combated by deploying the widest, most sensitive vocabulary in our search for the precise, concise term – as George Orwell so potently demonstrated by showing the wholly opposite effects of restriction and standardization of language in *Nineteen eighty-four* (Orwell, 1949). There:

> The whole aim of Newspeak is to narrow the range of thought [...] every year fewer words, and the range of consciousness always a little smaller. [...] What was required was short clipped words of unmistakable meaning which [...] roused the minimum of echoes in the speaker's mind. [...] The smaller the area of choice, the smaller the temptation to take thought.

Articles on **bias in indexing** that have appeared in *The Indexer* are:

Bias in indexing [on John Oldmixon / Laurence Echard].
    M. D. Anderson. **9**(1), 27–30
Bias in indexing [on Bernard Levin]. **12**(1), 54
Bias in indexing [on book on prisons]. Hazel K. Bell. **13**(2), 106
Indexes past: *Alps and sanctuaries of Piedmont and the Canton Ticino.*
    13(4), 259
Misrepresentation: passim. Hazel K. Bell. **14**(1), 56
A Shavian index. Hazel K. Bell. **15**(1), 26–7
Sisterly indexing [on Dale and Lynne Spender]. **15**(3), 167
Bias in indexing and loaded language. Hazel K. Bell. **17**(3), 173–7
Scholarly search for the truth. M. Mallory & G. Moran. **19**(2), 99–101
Whom should we aim to please? Hazel K. Bell. **20**(1), 3–5
'Let no damned Tory' [John Oldmixon / Laurence Echard]. **33**(2), 82–4

---

7.   All in order:
a proper arrangement

Having reduced the text to discrete elements, we must reunite and assemble these in index order, editing and grouping. We have produced the pieces of our jigsaw, which must now be fitted together: we must organize the arrangement of these long sequences of subheadings. Computers can arrange them for indexers in alphabetical order or by page number. Neither is appropriate for indexes to biographies, where subheadings may best be arranged chronologically or in some logical, ad hoc system, as in Latham's index to Pepys (see below).

Alphabetization

For the system of alphabetization to be used, letter-by-letter or word-by-word, Neil Fisk, while maintaining that word-by-word order should not be used for indexing 'technical or scientific texts or large reference works' for which he considered it 'demonstrably disastrous', drew a clear distinction between such firm, documentary texts and 'memoirs, biographies, autobiographies and histories'. He called indexers of the latter type of books 'stout defenders of the word-by-word method', as 'letter-by-letter indexing can occasionally separate items that ought to be kept together' (Fisk, 1968). We may choose to arrange our main headings so; and the treatment of hyphens, symbols, numbers and abbreviations can be left to our Standards to determine. The crucial question in soft, narrative indexing at this point is how to arrange the subheadings, especially in the long entries: a much-disputed one.

Subheadings

Latham enthuses about this stage of the indexer's work (Latham and Latham, 1980):

> Big indexes [...] are a minor art-form and combine the pleasures of a jig-saw puzzle with those of a Victorian paper game. You play around with hundreds of page references so that they fit into a design.

There are four possible methods of arrangement of subheadings: (1) page-order occurrence; (2) chronological; (3) alphabetical; or (4) thematic/classificatory. Michael Gordon (1983) considered them all:

> As to subheadings – is there any virtue in arranging them alphabetically, other than neatness of presentation? [...] Page order seems to me to make the handling of the book, turning to and from the index and text, much simpler than the alphabetical arrangement. [...] The virtue of page order is, of course, partly lost where there is more than one page to an entry; but alphabetical order seems to me to have no virtue to lose. [...] I prefer chronological order for histories and biographies so that, for example, people who are entered achieve education before death. Chronology cannot be consistently maintained since it does not cover such concepts as character or writings; these are probably better entered in separate paragraphs, the arrangement of which can be in page order.

Page order

By far the simplest method for the working indexer is just to leave the subheadings in the order they occur in the text, unedited. With luck, the development of the text in narratives will be chronological, so that as we work through the book, adding entry after entry, the result untampered-with will be in order of occurrence in the action. Edwin Holmstrom (1965) advocated this arrangement for 'a narrative literary work':

> The plan which is easiest for the indexer to follow, and which also is convenient to the user of the index, is to put the

subheadings in the same sequence as they occur in the text. [...] This is a satisfactory arrangement for the purpose, because in a narrative work the order of the page numbers will generally correspond with the time order of the events reported and this is as helpful an order as any for the reader to follow when searching for whichever items having a 'wanted relevance' he requires.

This not only is the easiest way in which to leave each block of subheads, but can be delegated to the computer to carry out. It has a certain justifying logic, and is the method used in the Wheatley-winning index to the biography of *'Clemency' Canning* (Piggott, 1991). (The entry for the main character there, though, is divided into paragraphs: CAREER [four columns, ending mentioned briefly]; APPEARANCE; CHARACTER; OPINIONS.) Complications may arise with this ordering of subheadings when later page references are added to an earlier heading which fits them also; runs of references become in order of occurrence of the first number in each run, constantly going back to start again at an earlier point for the next subhead.

But there may well be snarls in this fairly chronological sequence, if, for instance, the first chapter reviews the whole story, or opens with a climactic moment of the biographee's career – even his funeral – or there are recapitulations of earlier events, or developments or themes are successively retraced through a period. Wellisch observes, 'Alas, frightful examples of pseudo-chronological arrangement of subheadings in page order are all too often found' (1991). The results of this method have sometimes been scarifyingly castigated, as when Bernard Levin devoted an entire *Times* article to 'the full, almost heroic awfulness' of the index to Ian Ker's biography of Cardinal Newman (Clarendon Press, 1988, 762 pages), complaining particularly that 'the hundreds of references [under the entry for the main character] are not in alphabetical order at all, but only in the order in which they appear in the book' (Levin, 1989).

An extensive page order/chronological entry for the main character is found in the index to *Vanessa Bell* by Frances Spalding (Ticknor & Fields, 1983). The text is of 363 pages; the index, 13 (in two columns), of which over two and a half are occupied by the entry for Bell, Vanessa. It is divided into paragraphs headed: LIFE (2 pages); RELATIONSHIPS (half a column); ART (over half a page). The subheadings, each chronologically (= page order) arranged, repeat the exact terminology of the text, with no attempt at condensation or grouping together of like instances (nor any abbreviations). They include, *sic*:

> grubs among books; cajoles Virginia; bawdiness; changing taste; learns to absorb suffering; in rebellious mood; suspicious of insincerity; her sensuality aroused; growing taste for strong colour; explains Bloomsbury's lack of prescience; callous to Roger; inspires Virginia; moves away from abstraction; horrified by Omega-decorated flat; doubt and reassurance; catches moth for Julian; weeds furiously at Charleston; free, careless, airy, indifferent; edginess with Virginia; dreaded; acute delight in seeing Julian in Roger's company; stunned by Roger's death; declares politics and art don't mix

This is surely over-egging of the pudding, leaving hardly a need to read the full(er) text. Such a dutiful, un-reformatted digest of the whole, seeming determined to lose no golden word, suggests an author's own index. (Two pages of acknowledgements in this book do not include mention of the index.)

Reviewing Nigel Nicolson's autobiography, *Long life* (Putnam's, 1998), Penelope Fitzgerald (1998) observes that he arranges it 'rather oddly – not in order of time but thematically, with chapters allocated (more or less) to his many occupations' (Fitzgerald, 1998).

Chronology observed

True chronological order, though, achieved by diligent editing, faithfully reproduces the actual order of events as they occurred in the characters' lives, not just as they are recorded in the text. This should make it simple for the reader to locate items, whose order of occurrence should be guessable if not already known. A. S. Byatt (2001) writes:

> The biographer, Jenny Uglow, speaks with pleasure of good chronological guides to lives, to be found within indexes, and the sheer unuseful irritation produced by rendering these subentries in alphabetical form – beginning with 'Aunt Amy's visit' not because it came early, but because it begins with A.

Knight preaches, of chronological subheadings in histories and biographies: 'Their order in the index must be kept strictly chronological, irrespective of the page-reference order in the text' (1979). Chronologically arranged entries, moreover, are stylistically pleasing: they can be read through themselves as minor narratives, forming coherent wholes and conveying the tenor of the text. Two famous examples of such narrative index entries come from R. C. Latham's 1983 index to Pepys's diary (Latham and Matthews, 1983), and F. A. Pottle's of 1950 to Boswell's *London Journal* (Boswell, 1950) (quoted here without page numbers):

> BAGWELL − , wife of William: her good looks; P plans to seduce; visits; finds her virtuous; and modest; asks P for place for her husband; P kisses; she grows affectionate; he caresses; she visits him; her resistance collapses in alehouse; amorous encounters with: at her house [...]
>
> Lewis, Mrs (Louisa), actress. JB to call Louisa in journal; receives JB; JB visits; JB's increased feeling for; JB discusses love with; JB anticipates delight with; JB lends two guineas to; disregards opinion of world; discusses religion with JB; JB entreats to be kind; uneasiness of discourages JB; JB declares passion for; promises to make JB blessed; [...] makes assignation with JB; consummation with JB interrupted; [...] JB likes better and better; JB's felicity delayed; [...] JB afraid of a rival; JB feels coolness for; [...] JB incredulous at infection from; JB enraged at perfidy of; [...] JB asks his two guineas back [...]

The terms chosen for these subheadings are most felicitous; the arrangement is perfect. Note too the profusion of prepositions, aiding the natural narrative flow.

The major difficulty in arranging subheadings chronologically is what to do with successive but separate references to the same topic: someone's personal appearance at various stages of their life; repeated visits to the same place; an annual ceremony. Grouping these together will lose the chronological sequence of the whole, constantly jerking forward and back to start again; leaving them in their correct moment in time will necessitate frequent, spaceconsuming repetition of the subheading as well as separation of the references.

Blocks of subheadings may be chronologically divided into groups or stages of life, rather than individually specified, giving one subheading to five or so co-occurring references. Easiest of all is to subdivide into years by date – these take little space, are tidy divisions, and easy to establish. But this division is best used when the reader may be expected to have enough relevant knowledge for the dates alone to convey anything of the likely events covered in that period. Except for histories, only a few special cases, such as 1914–18 or 1939–45, would convey something to the user without needing glosses or added details; but in biographies dates of special significance in the life in question suggest little without qualification. Subheadings adducing the known in this way are easier to compile than those that need explanation, as subheadings probably will, in the private lives recounted in biographies.

Collocation also achieves a classification that may be helpful. Latham explained, of his index to Pepys (Latham and Latham, 1980):

> One of the principles of the design was to gather as many references as possible into clusters – under general terms such as FOOD, DRINK, DRESS and so on – so that the Index could enable the diary to serve as a book of reference.

Bella Weinberg is opposed to page/chronological order for biographical indexes (Weinberg, 1989), suggesting: 'Indexes should complement the logical arrangement of a book rather than replicate it', and recommending the application of the principles of chain indexing to justify entries such as

> Birth: [Biographee].

Stephen Leacock (1942) complained that 'a simple listing of the facts as found in the text will produce an illogical order so that "many events of his life get shifted out of their natural order"'. For example:

> John Smith: born. p. 1: born again. p. 1: […] mother born. p. 4: mother's family leave Ireland. p. 5: still leaving it. p. 6: school. p. 7: dies of pneumonia and enters Harvard. p. 9: eldest son born. p. 10: marries. p. 11: […]

The alphabetical way

Alphabetical arrangement of subheadings in indexes to biographies appears to have some advantages; sometimes, even, reviewers (such as Levin) deplore its not having been used. Neil Fisk (1968) pleaded for it:

> I do sometimes wish that these indexes ['of biographies and other such works'] too could be alphabetical throughout, subheadings as well as the main headings. [...] I often think I could find [examples of the more bizarre assertions or odder acts of Sir George Sitwell (in Sir Osbert Sitwell's autobiography, *Left hand, right hand* [1945])] more quickly if the group of entries under his name were arranged alphabetically.

Carey, though, defended the opposite case, writing of his own indexing of *Haldane of Cloan*:

> Why must subheadings *always*, according to some authorities, be alphabetical? May not rule just occasionally give way to common sense? (Carey, 1961)

As alphabetical order will almost certainly be the arrangement of the main headings, there is a certain elegant consistency in carrying the same principle through to the subheadings. Also, computers can manage the entire operation this way. It is admirably suitable for works where the subheadings are those obviously to be expected: climate / geography / history / population of a country, for instance.

There are disadvantages, though, to alphabetical arrangement of subheads in biographies. Their wording may not be the expected version, in such a subjective field, and the keywords in run-on narrative style may not be brought to the front. This order may also lead to absurd variance from both chronology and logic, as in Leacock's example above. Douglas Matthews explains his reasons for usually avoiding alphabetical arrangements under main headings (Matthews, personal communication, 1991):

> The terms (unlike scientific ones, which are precise and specific) are adopted, even arbitrary, and so seem no more helpful to the reader than any other order. To take a hypothetical instance: in a book on Cromwell, his warts might be the subject of comment;

and the indexer might make a subheading under that word. On the other hand he may prefer to put all physical features together under APPEARANCE or PHYSICAL FEATURES or DISFIGUREMENTS or SKIN CONDITION, and so the reader might not light on the reference to warts, overlooking the form used.

For the thematic/classificatory method, see next chapter.

Articles on **alphabetization** that have appeared in *The Indexer* are:

Memorandum on the method of alphabetization laid down by the Draft British Standard for Indexes. Neil R. Fisk. **3**(3), 93–4

Law and order, alphabetical. Michael Gordon. **13**(4), 255–6

The origins of the order of the letters. David Diringer. **6**(2), 54–8

The alphabetization of prepositions in indexes. Hans H. Wellisch. **12**(2), 90–2

Alphabetization in indexes. J. Hartley, L. Davies & P. Burnhill. **12**(3), 149–53

An alternative index. Hazel K. Bell. **25**(4), 255–6

Facilitas inveniendi: the alphabetical index as a knowledge management tool. Helmut Zedelmaier. **25**(4), 235–42

Some early guidance on arrangement and cross-referencing in an index. H. B. Wheatley. C18:15

Alphabetico-specific indexing. Alan Walker. **36**(1), 9–13

---

8. Theme by theme

A reviewer of a biography referred to 'the first problem of the biographer, whether to follow a strict chronology or to pursue particular themes' (Briggs, 1990). The indexer of a biography has to make the same decision. This last, fourth way to arrange subheadings in narrative indexes requires more work than alphabetical, chronological, or page number order. It is the method adopted for the long entries in most of the indexes cited in this booklet. This is *logical* or *thematic* grouping of subheads, into paragraphs with such headings as FAMILY, CHARACTER, CAREER, RELATIONSHIPS, LETTERS, WORKS, as appropriate for each book (designated 'prime subheads' by Douglas Matthews). Within these sections, entries appear as further subheadings – in fact, they are sub-subs of the main headings. I use small capitals for the paragraph headings, to make them stand out.

Christopher Phipps (2012) recommends this method, suggesting that in biographies, subheadings under the name of the leading character 'comprise different types of terms, which can be classified into a range of categories, including: actions; characteristics; relationships; views; works'.

Douglas Matthews adopted this method in working on Peter Ackroyd's biography of Dickens (Matthews, personal communication, 1991):

> In this huge book I soon realized that it needed some order under DICKENS, CHARLES, because of his dominance in the text, and adopted an arrangement under his name into prime subheads: all designed to make it easier to use. Within these subdivisions the order is by occurrence within the text, which is generally chronological in such a narrative biography.

The note preceding the index to the biography of Anthony Eden begins:

With the exception of the entries for Anthony Eden and his immediate family, the arrangement of subheadings in the index is chronological, following the order in which subjects first occur in the text. Reference to the diaries, letters, relationships and views of those indexed are grouped at the end of the sequence of subheadings, in the entry for each person (James, 1988).

Examples of paragraphed subheadings

These are the paragraph headings used to divide the entries for the main characters in a selection of indexes to biographies:

Jane Austen by Claire Tomalin; Viking, 1998
AUSTEN, JANE: (first paragraph of family and early life); ADULT LIFE; RELATIONSHIPS; WRITINGS: LETTERS; NOVELS; VERSES (one-page entry)

A life of Gerald Brenan: the interior castle by J. Gathorne-Hardy; Sinclair-Stevenson, 1994
BRENAN, GERALD: (long first paragraph, biographical, with no heading); AWARDS; FINANCES; LIBRARY; PERSONAL CHARACTERISTICS; RELATIONSHIPS; WRITING; LETTERS; POETRY; PUBLISHED WORKS (one and a half pages)

Benjamin Britten: A Biography by Humphrey Carpenter; Faber and Faber, 1982
In the 23-page General Index: BRITTEN, [EDWARD] BENJAMIN: LIFE (4 columns); CHARACTER, ATTRIBUTES AND INTERESTS (3 columns). There is also a second, detailed, nearly 8-page 'Index of Britten's Works' (for more on this, see page 87).

Rich: the life of Richard Burton by Melvyn Bragg; Hodder & Stoughton, 1988
BURTON, RICHARD: CAREER; CHARACTERISTICS AND TASTES; ACTING; WEALTH; RELATIONSHIPS; MARRIAGES; WRITINGS (nearly one page, triple-column)

'Clemency' Canning by Michael Maclagan; Macmillan, 1962
CAREER; APPEARANCE; CHARACTER; OPINIONS (three pages)

Winston S. Churchill [...] vol. 2, Young statesman, 1901–1919 by
Randolph S. Churchill; Heinemann, 1967
CHURCHILL, WINSTON: CHARACTERISTICS; EDUCATION; FINANCES;
HEALTH; HOBBIES; MILITARY CAREER; POLITICAL INTERESTS

Dickens by Peter Ackroyd; Christopher Sinclair-Stevenson, 1990
DICKENS, CHARLES: BIOGRAPHY AND PERSONAL LIFE (3+ columns);
CHARACTERISTICS (2 columns); HEALTH; IDEAS, BELIEFS AND OPINIONS; LITERARY
LIFE AND ENDEAVOURS (1.5 columns); PORTRAITS; PUBLIC READINGS; SPEECHES;
THEATRICALS; TRAVELS ABROAD (total 5.5 pages)

Anthony Eden by Robert Rhodes James; Weidenfeld & Nicolson, 1986
EDEN, ANTHONY: four personal paragraphs come first – ANCESTRY;
EARLY LOVE AFFAIRS; MARRIAGE; CHILDREN; then seven paragraphs in
chronological order, each representing a stage of Eden's political
career, including CAREER; EARLY INTEREST IN POLITICS; FOREIGN SECRETARY;
then TRIBUTES, HONOURS AND AWARDS, BROADCASTS, SPEECHES, WRITINGS
(JOURNALISM / FAMILY LETTERS / MEMOIRS / three book titles); then, in
alphabetical order, seven personal paragraphs – APPEARANCE AND DRESS,
ART COLLECTION, CHARACTER AND PERSONALITY; FINANCES; HEALTH; PERSONAL
RELATIONSHIPS; RELATIONSHIPS WITH PARLIAMENTARY COLLEAGUES GENERALLY;
PERSONAL AND OFFICIAL PAPERS; BIOGRAPHER'S ASSESSMENT OF (total 33
paragraphs)

T. S. Eliot by Peter Ackroyd; Hamish Hamilton, 1984
ELIOT, THOMAS STEARNS: BIOGRAPHY (nearly 4 columns,
subheadings in page order); CHARACTER (1.5 columns, subheadings in
alphabetical order); OPINIONS .75 column, alphabetical order); WRITINGS
(six columns, subheadings in alphabetical order, some with sub-subs in
alphabetical order)

T. S. Eliot: a memoir by Robert Sencourt; Garnstone Press, 1971
ELIOT, THOMAS STEARNS: (first a half-column-long paragraph
of biographical events, with subheadings in chronological order);
RELATIONSHIPS (in alphabetical order); RELIGION (with subheadings –
early views, interests; conversion to C. of E.; baptism, confirmation;
as Anglican); CHARACTERISTICS; RECREATIONS; INTERESTS (cats; Eastern

thought; literary; philosophy; poetical; politics); PROSE WORKS; PLAYS; POEMS; LETTERS (total one and a half pages)

Gladstone by Roy Jenkins; Macmillan, 1995
GLADSTONE, WILLIAM EWART: ACTIVITIES AND RECREATIONS; CHARACTERISTICS; EDUCATION; FINANCES; HEALTH; HONOURS; INTELLECTUAL INTERESTS; PERSONAL; POLITICAL LIFE; (nearly four columns); RELIGIOUS LIFE; TRAVELS; WORKS (total over four pages)

The Life of Samuel Johnson, LLD by James Boswell; Clarendon Press, 1934–64
JOHNSON, SAMUEL: ('begins with a chronological list of the principal events of the subject's life, with page-references; there follow four numbered alphabetical series'): I GENERAL; II LETTERS; III LETTERS WRITTEN TO JOHNSON; IV 'WRITINGS (INCLUDING DIARIES …) AND MATTERS RELATING TO THEM' (17 paragraphs)

John Keats: a life by Stephen Coote; Hodder & Stoughton, 1995
KEATS, JOHN: BIOGRAPHY; PERSONAL; RELICS; WORKS (one and a half pages)

John Maynard Keynes, Vol. 2: The Economist as Saviour, 1920–1937 by Robert Skidelsky; Macmillan, 1992
KEYNES, JOHN MAYNARD: CAREER AND ACTIVITIES; CHARACTERISTICS; PERSONAL AND PRIVATE LIFE; VIEWS AND OPINIONS; SEE UNDER TITLE FOR INDIVIDUAL PUBLICATIONS BY JMK (one page)

Arthur Koestler: The Homeless Mind by David Cesarani; Heinemann, 1998
KOESTLER, ARTHUR: (long first paragraph, biographical, with no heading); PERSONAL; RELATIONSHIPS; REPUTATION AND STATUS; LECTURES; WORKS (ending see also titles of publications in which works by AK appeared)

Katherine Mansfield: A Secret Life by Claire Tomalin; Viking, 1987
'MANSFIELD, KATHERINE' (KATHERINE MANSFIELD BEACHAMP): (more than 3 columns with no subheading); PHYSICAL APPEARANCE; HEALTH; CHARACTER; WORKS

Indexing biographies

Michelangelo: a biography by George Bull; Viking, 1995
MICHELANGELO (Michelagniolo Buonarroti): APPEARANCE; ARTISTIC
CAREER; ARTISTIC TRAINING; BIRTH AND EARLY YEARS; CRITICS OF; DEATH;
FAMILY; FINANCES; FRIENDSHIPS; HEALTH; HOMES; MILITARY ENGINEER; PATRONS;
PERSONAL CHARACTERISTICS; POLITICS; RELIGION AND: WORKS (ARCHITECTURAL);
WORKS (PAINTINGS AND DRAWINGS); WORKS (SCULPTURES); WRITINGS (total
seven-column entry)

Sean O'Casey: a life by Garry O'Connor; Hodder & Stoughton, 1988
O'CASEY, SEAN: (first paragraph, general biography and career, no
heading); ATTITUDES; RELATIONSHIPS; WORKS (over one and a half pages –
three columns).

Pepys: a biography by Richard Ollard; Hodder & Stoughton 1974
PEPYS, SAMUEL: PERSONAL LIFE; WORK AND CAREER; QUALITIES AND
CHARACTER; HEALTH; FINANCES AND REWARDS; INTERESTS AND TASTES;
RESIDENCES; POLITICS; RELIGION; JOURNEYS; WRITING

Bertrand Russell by Caroline Moorehead; Sinclair-Stevenson, 1992
RUSSELL, BERTRAND: BIOGRAPHY; CHARACTERISTICS; ATTITUDES, BELIEFS
AND PLEASURES; WRITINGS (two and a half pages)

Bernard Shaw Volume I 1856–1898: The Search for Love by Michael
Holroyd; Chatto & Windus, 1988
SHAW, GEORGE BERNARD: (a two-column long first paragraph,
biographical, with no heading); SHAW ON (topics listed alphabetically);
SHAW'S LETTERS AND COMMUNICATIONS TO (recipients listed alphabetically,
with topics as subheadings – more than two columns); WORKS (nearly
two columns)

Stalin by Edvard Radzinsky; Hodder & Stoughton, 1995
STALIN: BIOGRAPHY; PERSONAL; RELATIONSHIPS; WRITINGS (nearly one page)

The order in which these paragraphs are arranged varies; it is not
necessarily alphabetical. Within the paragraphs, also, different orders of
subheadings may be adopted – some alphabetical, some chronological.
In his index to *Haldane of Cloan*, Carey gave Haldane, Richard Burdon

'an entry of his own, in two parts, the first comprising about a dozen of the main events of his career, in chronological order; the second headed *Personal traits* and listed in alphabetical order' (Carey, 1961).

For the Dickens index, Douglas Matthews uses order of occurrence with the paragraphs headed:

BIOGRAPHY AND PERSONAL LIFE; HEALTH; LITERARY LIFE AND ENDEAVOURS; PORTRAITS; PUBLIC READINGS; and THEATRICALS

– each of which is set run-on; and alphabetical order under:

CHARACTERISTICS; IDEAS, BELIEFS AND OPINIONS; SPEECHES (by place given); and TRAVELS ABROAD.

The alphabetically arranged paragraphs are set indented, including their own sub-subheadings and many cross-references.

Of Powell's index to Boswell, de Beer (1967) writes:

the entries for London, Oxford, Pope and Shakespeare are each divided into two or more alphabetical series [...] the entry for the *Lives of the poets* [...] is divided into five somewhat discursive series relating to the growth and fortunes of the book. The entries for Burke and Goldsmith are each divided into two alphabetical sections, using heavy type initials. [...] those for Boswell and Johnson [...] begin with a chronological list of the principal events of the subject's life.

Tracing the themes

Each long entry in an index represents a single strand through the book, which must be individually traced in turn when that entry is edited, going back through the whole work looking for the overall pattern of the references to the one person. Reading the book thus repeatedly and selectively, one is working in the way described by A. S. Byatt as that of A-level literature study (Byatt, 1978):

One was required to discuss the function of characters in the plot, and [...] what extra individuality they had, what intrinsic nature [...] the other thing [...] was trace recurrent images.

Tracing one major character and theme after another thus singly through a book to finalize its index entry reminds me of preparing for examinations on literature. This process is described by Thomas Hardy in his diary entry for 3 June 1882:

> as in looking at a carpet, by following one colour a certain pattern is suggested, by following another colour, another; so in life the seer should watch that pattern amid general things which his idiosyncracy moves him to observe, and describe that alone. (Hardy, 1882)

9. Mighty main characters

As the fish said, 'what water?'

It is, of course, in the treatment of the main character of a biography that the difficulties of long entries with multiple subheadings become most acute.

Leave it out?

Margie Towery (2017) comments, 'There is an old idea that the metatopic itself should never appear in the index, because if it did, you would have to index the whole book under that single main heading'. There have been distinguished advocates of the simple omission of such entries for biographies.

Gordon Carey denounced long entries for the main character of a biography as 'overloading', suggesting they should be omitted, or restricted to entries which could not go under any other heading, such as his birth, character, honours, rather than producing 'column after column after column of sub-entries, extending as likely as not to several pages – classified, perhaps, in three or four separate sections, but even so needing an auxiliary index to help you find any individual object of search' (Carey, 1963). He declared, 'When indexing a biography [...] I start with a predisposition against an individual entry for the central figure, primarily because the whole book is about him'. He applied this principle of dispersal in indexing *The memoirs of Lord Ismay*, and placed at the top of the index, 'as a form of shock-absorber', he tells us, this note (Carey, 1961):

> In order to avoid the difficulty and delay in reference induced by several pages of subheadings under the main heading, ISMAY, LORD, the author's activities have been indexed under the persons, places, institutions, etc. to which they relate, his name, wherever appropriate, being indicated by I.

Knight (1964) wrote approvingly of Carey's precepts, saying that his article:

> showed how utterly unnecessary were most of the subheadings which would normally clutter up the several pages of index devoted to a synopsis of his entire career; the vast majority could be far more conveniently placed, and were more likely to be looked for, under appropriate separate entries.

Margaret Anderson (1971) also quoted Carey with approval, recommending that:

> Under X's name in the index are placed only such personal matters as his birth, marriage, and death, his characteristics, hobbies, illnesses, and honours.

Colin Matthew abjured altogether an entry for the main character in his award-winning index, stating:

> An important preliminary decision was not to have an entry for Gladstone himself. This would have been so large as to be extremely difficult to navigate in, and would have repeated most of the other entries in the Subject Index. (Matthew, 1995)

The Wheatley Panel made no mention of this omission in making its award to this index. Likewise, Alan Walker made no entry for the main character in his medal-winning index to former Prime Minister John Howard's autobiography *Lazarus rising*, as reported on page 23.

Abrupt compromises between full index entries for the main character of biographies and none are shown in *Horace Walpole (1717–1797): A Biographical Study by Lewis Melville* (Hutchinson & Company, 1930), where this unusual entry appears:

> Walpole, Horace. The subject of this memoir.

And in the index to *Edmund Gosse: a literary landscape* by Ann Thwaite (OUP, 1985):

> Gosse, Edmund, see individual entries, e.g. ancestry, inaccuracy, etc.; also titles of his books

Similarly on these accurate but uncluttered lines is the entry in the Everyman, 1906 edition of *The diary of Samuel Pepys:*

PEPYS, SAMUEL, Vol. I: 1 January 1660–31 March 1664; Vol. II: 1 April 1664–30 June 1667; Vol. III: 1 July 1667–31 May 1669.

Chapter headings may prove suitable to use as subheadings for really broad divisions.

Knight even censured the first winner of the Wheatley Medal for including in the three-page entry for Lord Canning, divided into four sections, a four-column first section, CAREER, deeming it 'really unnecessary since it is practically a synopsis of the entire text' (Knight, 1964). Personally, as reader, I would welcome such a synopsis, easy to find one's way through.

Simple removal of entries from under the main character will not solve the problems of extended continuity and grouping of multiple subheadings as they apply to *other* major characters in the book. Elizabeth Pepys and James Boswell claimed nearly equal time with their heroes; even the entry for Elizabeth Taylor in Richard Burton's biography was divided into paragraphs headed: CAREER; RELATIONSHIPS; CHARACTERISTICS; WEALTH AND FILMS, in a nearly two-column entry for a secondary character. Spouses and colleagues can run the main characters of biographies close seconds, thirds and subsequents. Washing one's hands of the main character will solve the problem of voluminous subheadings under single entries only if extended so far as to omit all major topics and index only minor ones – hardly helpful.

There is an opposite tendency from the omission of an entry for the main character in a biography in its index, while fully treating all other characters – compared with those who give full detailed breakdown for the main character, but leave strings for the rest. An example of the second type is the index to Barbara Pym's diary, which has a full, detailed entry for Pym herself, but leaves long undifferentiated strings for Henry Harvey, Philip Larkin, Robert Liddell, Oxford, Richard Roberts, Robert Smith, and Hilary Walton, all of whom are provided with glosses rather than subheadings (Pym, 1985). Equally determined that no reference to the main character shall be missed seems the indexer (/autobiographer?)

of Winston S. Churchill's *My Early Life* (Hamlyn, 1930). His entry, more than a column long, concludes with a single line:

and *passim.*

Carey suggested that most entries for the main character could go under other headings – for the hero's marriage, you look for his wife's name in the index, which will have become the same as his (Carey, 1961). But what of other close relationships, with people of different, unknown names – how to locate these? Knight complained that 'in the carefully compiled American index' to *Boswell in search of a wife* 'it is not pretty to find' 38 references to catching, escaping from, or being treated for, the pox, under BOSWELL, and that 'these had better been relegated to an entry under the letter V' (Knight, 1966). But if the reader did not already know what ailed him, they would not think to consult V for details of Boswell's health and sickness. Transferring the main character's references to other entries will indeed avoid long cumulations, but, like alphabetical arrangement of subheadings, will be helpful *only* to those who already know exactly what subjects they should look for, and how they will be expressed.

Piggott (1991), discussing the Maclagan index to the Canning biography, suggests:

> If the entry under the main character is very long, pin-pointing a specific topic, even when category headings have been used, can be difficult. It seems to me that double-entry is the only solution.

However, there are those who see much virtue in a long, detailed entry for the main character. Christopher Phipps (2012) suggests:

> Done well, a leading character's index entry can provide a really useful and easily navigable – even readable – synopsis of their life. It can also pull together scattered mentions of their attributes and characteristics which build into a cogent and accessible thumbnail sketch that might not readily be found elsewhere in the text.

Do Mi Stauber (2004) designates the main subject of a text the metatopic, identifying it as 'the structural center of the index: every single heading [...] will be implicitly related to it'. An index structure to cope with this is suggested by Towery (2017):

> I view the metatopic main heading as a useful place for any reader [...] to start an index search. [...] The metatopic main heading can be a window into the structure of the index and thus the text. Within this key entry array, I generally place two kinds of information: (1) subheadings that gather disparate bits of information that may not serve as main entries themselves (alternatively, some or all of the subheadings may also be double-posted to main headings, depending) and (2) cross-references to the most important main headings in the book.

Hero-treatment

Editing the entry for the main character in a biography I always leave to the last – irrespective of his initial – dealing with this when I have acquired maximum familiarity with the text by finalizing all the other entries. Settling the main character's entry usually entails trailing right through the book again, tracing this major theme.

The paragraph headings used for the entries for the main characters in twenty-two biographies are given on pages 69–72; for Charles Dickens, on pages 70, 73, 86 and 99; for Samuel Pepys, on pages 64, 65, 72 and 100–1. Here are some further examples.

An interesting and complex treatment of the main character is found in the 21-page index to *Berlioz: volume I: the making of an artist* by David Cairns (Deutsch, 1989; 563 pages). It is an original and ingenious index, whose author clearly knows just where he wishes his emphasis placed, and which must result from close study and analysis of the text. The indexer receives prominent credit: Professor G. D. West. The entry for 'Berlioz, Hector (HB)' takes over four pages, set run-on, divided into headed (in italics) paragraphs, some having their own subheadings. Here are some of these:

> *America, Asia, and the South Seas, HB's lifelong passion for;*
> *Anatomy, HB's early interest in* (one page-reference only);
> *Ancestry* (19–21); *Appearance; Birth* (one page ref.); *Branchu,*

> *Mme, influence on HB; Character* (subheadings alphabetically
> arranged after the first entry, 'recollections'); *Childhood*
> (nothing known up to the age of 12 years – one page ref.);
> *Composers influenced by HB* (alphabetically arranged); *Early
> instruction in music; Education; Father, HB's relationship with*
> (18-line entry with chronological arrangement of subheadings);
> *Ill-health; Influences on HB – literature* (43 lines); *Influences
> on HB – music* (36 lines); *Instruments, HB's knowledge of and
> ability to play; Journalism; Law, HB refuses to study instead of
> medicine* (two references); *Love Life* (this paragraph employs
> the only bold type in the index, for the names of five ladies, in
> alphabetical order, each with her array of sub-subheadings);
> *Works by HB – music, complete, fragmentary, and not extant*
> (nearly three columns)

A fuller critique of this index appears in *The Indexer* (Bell, 1990).

Moral desperado: a life of Thomas Carlyle by Simon Heffer
(Weidenfeld & Nicolson 1995) has 383 pages of text and a 14-page
index. (I have been unable to trace the name of the indexer – as so sadly
often.) The entry in the index for CARLYLE, THOMAS (entered *sic*, in
full capitals) fills three pages. It consists of 40 subheadings, indented,
in alphabetical order, many of them followed by several subheadings,
set run-on, also alphabetically. Some sample entries (without page
numbers here) are:

> birth and early years; accent; appearance; biographies of;
> correspondence and papers see …; employments (five
> sub-subheadings); finances (14); health (17); literary style (18);
> personal characteristics (ambition; authoritarian; earnestness;
> entertainingly ill-natured; exaggeration; ingratitude; intolerance;
> sarcasm; self-pity; selfishness; sense of humour; sensitivity;
> shopping disliked; shyness; thoughtlessness towards Jane;
> unaffected by praise or censure; ungraciousness; want of
> elegance; as a youth; *see also above* interests); personal
> philosophy (16 sub-subheadings); political philosophy (a third
> of a column); religious views (a quarter-column); reputation
> during life (quarter-column); reputation following death (5
> sub-subheadings); works (a full column).

The biography, *Cyril Connolly: a nostalgic life* by Clive Fisher (Macmillan, 1995), has what seems an interesting and original treatment of the main character in the index. First, the entry for Connolly, Cyril Vernon, which is over a page long, is made conspicuous by leaving line spaces before and after that entry, just as one does between alphabetical sections of an index, making this entry into a section on its own – unexceptionably, it seems to me.

Then, while the rest of the index is set with all subheadings run-on, Connolly's own entry is an exception to this. His entry is divided into paragraphs, with each indented paragraph (sub)heading followed by its own run-on subheadings (that is, sub-subs to the main heading). These are ordered chronologically for the first paragraph heading, 'Life'; alphabetically for all the rest. Here is a list of the paragraph headings, as they are set, with some of their attendant subs:

> life: family background; birth; childhood; [...] 60th birthday; 70th birthday; illness and death [19 lines of run-on subheads]
> appearance
> art collection
> book collection
> dress
> entertaining
> finances [16 lines of run-on subheads]
> health
> homes [13 lines of subheads]
> honours [2 lines]
> lifestyle: bachelor flat; country style; dreams; gardening; home decoration; pets; servants; South of France
> love affairs: Anne Dunn; Betty Mossop; Bobbie Longden; Caroline Blackwood; Diana; Elaine Tynan; Janetta Woolley; [...] schoolboys; [...] Sonia Orwell; Texas professor's wife [12 lines]
> politics
> wartime
> works (completed and projected) [nearly a column of subheads]

There is, moreover, another unusual feature in the layout of this entry. All the turnover (wrap-around) lines are run full out left; only the paragraph headings are indented. The spaces before these break up the block of text and make them easy to spot. Much space is saved in this way, as otherwise most of the lines of these two-plus columns would have had to be double-indented as sub-subheadings. The line spaces before and after this main entry help it to stand out as a separate section with a layout of its own. (The indexer, presumably responsible for such a splendid initiative, receives no acknowledgement in the volume.)

There are long and complex entries for the main (literary) character in both volumes of Brian Boyd's biography: *Vladimir Nabokov: the Russian years* and *Vladimir Nabokov: the American years* (Chatto & Windus, 1990; 1992). They have respectively 582 and 758 pages of text, each provided with a 25-page index. The entries for the main character in both extend over more than six pages. The heading in the index:

Nabokov, Vladimir Vladimirovich (1899–1977)

is followed each time by its own prefatory note:

(entries are arranged within the categories: Art and Thought; Life and Character; Works)

The sections are arranged alphabetically under these headings, set run-on, with a new paragraph for each new initial letter. Thus, in the Russian volume:

Art and Thought: [nearly two pages]
– afterlife: and father's death; – art: and the beyond, and generosity of life, as image on limits of consciousness transcended, ...
– the beyond: early attempts to render; – biography ...
– causation; – censorship; – chess ...
– death: as possible transcending of prison of self ...
– emigration, Russian, as subject ...

Life and Character: [two pages]
– as actor: ...
– birth of ...
– at Cambridge
– as dancer

Works: [over three pages]
- *Ada*: composition of, sources of, 'The Texture of Time' ...
- 'Bachman': German serialization of;
- 'A Bad Day';
- *Bend Sinister* ...
- *Camera Obscura*: composition of, Czech translation of, English translation of ...

And in the American volume –

Art and Thought: [one page]
- aesthetics; afterlife; America, hesitation to use as milieu in fiction; America, as theme in autobiography; ...
- censorship ...
- death ...
- 'enchantment' ...
Life and Character: [a little over two pages]
- accomplishment, sense of; airplanes, wariness of ...
Works: [three and a quarter pages]
- *Ada*: analysis of ...
- 'The Ballad of Longwood Glen'
- *Camera Obscura*.

Lolita and *Pale Fire* are each accorded two thirds of a column.

Quentin Bell's two-volume *Virginia Woolf* was published by the Hogarth Press in 1972, and as a single paperback publication by Triad/ Paladin in 1987. Volume I, 'Virginia Stephen', there runs from page 1 to 216; volume 2, 'Mrs Woolf', from a new page 1 to 259; then come reference lists and indexes for both volumes: 28 pages of indexes. The entry for Woolf, Virginia, takes one and a half pages of the first index, two of the second. Both parts are divided into numbered paragraphs, the subheadings within them set run-on in order of occurrence in the text.

The paragraph headings of the first are: I – *Life and Opinions*; II – *Literary Work*; of the second: I – *Descriptions of her person, occupations and character*; II – *Pathography*; III – *Literary work* (with nine lines following *see also*); IV – *Literary friendships* (four lines following *see also*); V – *Other Personal Relationships* (seven lines); VI – *Public affairs*; VII – *General* (from social trials of her engagement to thanks for butter).

Articles on the indexing of the **main character in a biography** that have appeared in *The Indexer* are:

Indexing a biography [Professor Soddy]. L. E. C. Hughes. **1**(4), 111
No room at the top. G. V. Carey. **2**(3), 120–3
'Clemency' Canning. G. N. Knight. **4**(1), 19–20/29
Indexing the life of Sir Winston Churchill. G. N. Knight. **5**(2), 58–63
Indexing biographies: the main character. Hazel K. Bell. **17**(1), 43–4
Authors as their own indexers ['Clemency' Canning]. Mary Piggott. **17**(3), 161–6
Distortion and mutilation – it can happen to us [Charles Dickens]. Hazel K. Bell, **18**(1), 40–1
An indexer's life of Johnson. Christopher Phipps. **30**(3), 114–19
Navigating *The English friend*. Susan Curran. **30**(3), 119–24

10.   The works

Listing volumes

There are particular difficulties in indexing books about the lives of those who themselves produce literary or musical works. Douglas Matthews, indexing a 44-volume edition of the writings of Daniel Defoe (Pickering and Chatto) that included several histories and memoirs, took this approach:

> Works by authors other than Defoe appear under the author's name, but Defoe's own works, when cited, appear directly under title. I believe that distributing his titles in this way makes for greater clarity particularly when sub-dividing his individual works, whereas listing them all under his name would make for a rather clumsy block of entries all in one place. Book titles all appear in italic, and to distinguish Defoe's works from other italicized headings (such as periodicals) I add the tag (DD) to identify the work as Defoe's. (Matthews, 2004)

Titles

The first problem is whether to disperse titles through the index or group them under the author's name. I prefer classification, if feasible: the amalgamated list is itself informative, and indeed, reference to his productions should appear in the author's entry, as an aspect of his working life and thought. Knight, though, chose a different course:

> For those of [Churchill's] works that are quoted or referred to in the text the reader is cross-referenced to the entries under their titles. (1966)

In what order to list amalgamated titles is a moot point. With an author whose many works are well known I would choose to list them alphabetically, as being titles familiar to the reader, who will probably expect to find them in alphabetical sequence. For an author of few books, though, not well known, each of which represents a career stage and a period of their life – research, residence in the location of the book, perhaps, the sustained business of the writing, publication, reviews and repercussions – chronological sequence seems more appropriate. In Richard Burton's biography, film and play titles were career stages.

De Beer (1967) comments on this issue:

> I suppose the only practical course for useful guidance is to guess at what lies between the titles that 'every schoolboy knows' and those that will be required only by specialists who are bound to know the authors.

It may prove necessary to give works their own individual entries, cross-referred from the author's entry, to allow an extra level of subheadings for them. As well as being productions of the writer's intelligence and industry, books may have a literary history requiring their own subheadings: progress of composition; publication; reviews and repercussions; reprints; distribution of copies; dramatization. These are the subheadings in Matthews' *Dickens* index under the main one, *Christmas Carol, A*:

> boyhood reading in; CD reads; character of Tiny Tim in; and Cornish tin mines; dismissed by *Westminster Review*; Fancy in; on home; and money; origins; writing of; pirated; portrays Bayham Street house; profits; publication; quality; reality of characters in; religion in; success of

There are about three-quarters of a column of subheadings each under *Bleak House, David Copperfield,* and *Little Dorrit*; and half a column each under *Martin Chuzzlewit, Mystery of Edwin Drood, Oliver Twist, Our Mutual Friend, Pickwick Papers,* and *Tale of Two Cities*, in the Dickens book. The entries for Nabokov's chief works in the index to Brian Boyd's biography are long and much subdivided (see pages 82–3).

To avoid long paragraphs of cross-referenced titles listed under authors' entries, Leigh Priest gives the dispersed titles in bold type, with a *see* note at the bottom of the writer's entry giving instruction to look for the works in bold throughout the index (Priest, personal communication, 1992). Then, the author's books may be manifest in the biography also as sources – quoted or disputed, contrasted with other accounts of the events described. Books in books have many aspects.

The majority of the indexes cited on pages 69–72 have a subheading, works or writings under the entry for the main character – sometimes very long. As noted (page 69), in the volume *Benjamin Britten: A Biography* there is a second, detailed, nearly 8-page 'Index of Britten's Works'. In that, the entries for *Billy Budd*, *Death in Venice* and *The Turn of the Screw* each run to half a column, and *Peter Grimes* to more.

The index to John Eliot Gardiner's biography, *Music in the castle of heaven: a portrait of Johann Sebastian Bach* (Allen Lane, 2013) explains in detail its policy regarding the indexing of his works in a prefatory note:

> Musical compositions named in the index are generally filed under their composer. Those by J. S. Bach are arranged by genre and name under the heading Bach, Johann Sebastian, works, with the exception of the cantatas, the surviving Passions, and the *B Minor Mass*, which all receive major treatment in the book and have their own main heading in the index: 'cantatas of J. S. Bach', 'John Passion', 'Matthew Passion' and 'Mass in B Minor by J. S. Bach'.

The index to this biography runs to 29 pages: the main heading Bach, Johann Sebastian, man and musician is followed by two pages of subheadings; Bach, Johann Sebastian, works by nearly two pages; cantatas of J. S. Bach by four pages; 'John Passion', 'Matthew Passion' and 'Mass in B Minor by J. S. Bach' by one column each.

Christopher Phipps considered all the options for listing Dr Johnson's many works, and chose both to give (Phipps, 2012):

> individual index entries for the works in their own right; the entries on some titles themselves containing detailed subheading breakdowns covering matters of the work's origin, production, publication, revision and content. [...] With the detailed coverage included elsewhere in the index, it would therefore have been possible under the Johnson, Samuel: Works

subentry simply to have opted for see individual titles. This, though, optimistically presupposes that readers and index users will all be familiar with the titles covered in the text. It also misses another opportunity for the index to add further value to the editorial apparatus of the book. I therefore chose to provide a much fuller see reference listing the works individually by title. This also indicates the further index entries which bring together other works by Johnson in particular genres, such as poetry, political pamphlets, prayers, prefaces and introductions, reviews, sermons and translations, plus his contributions to specific named magazines; the cumulative whole thereby comprising a handy mini-bibliography of all the Johnson works discussed in the text.

Characters
Entries for characters in works of fiction may bring further problems. Forenames only may be given; or they may be always known as 'Little Em'ly', 'Little Nell'; what form of name to give for these? And where? Characters appearing in a single work may be listed under the title of that work – Ophelia under *Hamlet*, Fagin under *Oliver Twist* – but recurrent characters, such as Dorothy Sayers' Lord Peter Wimsey and Harriet Vane, may be best entered directly under their names. They should then be typographically distinguished from real people; if italic type is used to indicate illustrations, and bold for main entries, then quotation marks could indicate the fictionality of

'Bond, James'
'Wooster, Bertram'

The index (by Christine Shuttleworth) to Victoria Glendinning's biography of Anthony Trollope (Hutchinson, 1992) in addition to a long sub-entry, WORKS, under his own name, had a separate entry under C, characters in AT's WORKS, listing the many characters in his sequence of novels referred to in the biography, in alphabetical order (at the request of the biographer).

Letters

Letters written by the characters in biographies or histories, similarly, may be treated as indications of their developing relationships; examples of their literary, perhaps published, products; valued relics; or as sources for the narrative. The relevant sub-subheadings in two entries in my index to *Jane Austen* read:

> (under Austen, Jane)
> LETTERS: to Fanny Austen (niece); to James-Edward Austen-Leigh; to Anne Sharp; *see also under* Austen, Cassandra (sister); published; *and* other papers, posthumous disposal
> Austen-Leigh, James-Edward (nephew of JA): letters to: JA's, about writing; JA's last; father's, in JA's last illness

and in the index entry for Gerald Brenan in his biography:

> LETTERS [...]; publication considered; published; archived; *see also under* recipients

Under the entry for Winston Churchill himself in Knight's index, the preliminary note tells us:

> there are for several types of material cross-references only, e.g.:
> CHURCHILL, Winston Leonard Spencer, LETTERS from and to: *see under* the names of recipients and senders. (Bancroft, 1968)

11. Just mentioning ...

After all references worthy of the distinction and space of subheadings have duly received them, there are likely to remain for major entries lists of page references to minor mentions, too trivial for subheadings, but too many together, or just significant enough, not to be omitted altogether. This, of course, may result in the undifferentiated strings of page numbers that many indexers and critics condemn. Judy Batchelor (1983) wrote wittily about an index with subject headings 'attended by massed ranks of page-references':

> The total view, of handsome, unbroken blocks of greyish-black print on a whitish ground, offers an almost hypnotic design of severe restraint; it should prove ideal for library wallpaper in times of recession [rather than] the utilitarianism of 'reader-accessibility'.

For biographies, there is the problem of a multitude of minor mentions. Minor characters, relations or long-term friends or colleagues of the main character, may appear recurrently in the book, merely mentioned as constantly there in the background. The indexer must choose between omitting them; giving them a false impression of significance by according them subheadings; or letting them honestly appear as unqualified lists of minor mentions – and thus fall open to censure by index judges. I have myself been censured for compiling an index, to my own book, that was deemed to have 'too many undifferentiated locators' – all these were, indeed, mentions not significant enough to require subheadings, but too many for the subject to be omitted, and the strings the result of careful consideration by the author/indexer (Toole, 2007).

I find strings may well be justifiable, preferable to any of the alternative means of dealing with minor references detailed below.

Omission, *tout court*, I would deplore. Someone who appears twelve times through the book, as a minor, background figure on several occasions, does merit inclusion in the index. The twelve references together may achieve only the same scale of importance as one single main entry; but the name should then appear in the index, as having repeatedly appeared in the book. Perhaps even a single minor mention merits inclusion – 'If an author sees fit to name somebody who are we to ignore that person?' asks Ian Craine (2018).

Prefacing strings with the word *mentioned*, often advocated, seems pompous and overloading to me – such a long word in this context as to be paradoxically used! The use of *passim* similarly introduces an extra word where one is trying to minimize space taken. A happier solution is suggested in the prefatory note to Thornton's index to Dickens' letters:

> The word 'also' preceding a series of page numbers indicates that the references are minor and miscellaneous. (Thornton, 1965)

I was fascinated by Michael Brackney's suggestion of printing gray locators or superscript numerals to indicate minor mentions but – hardly surprisingly – it never caught on (Bell, 2008a).

Applying arithmetical principles to reduce a string of eleven such page numbers to an acceptable five by picking out some at random to receive unmerited distinction and prominence by subheading them could result in an unbalanced index, falsely suggesting to users that important passages will be found by turning to those references. There should be a true correspondence between the importance of a character or passage in the text, and the space it occupies in the index; subheadings should be accorded on the basis of the intrinsic importance of the entry, never merely to distinguish one unimportant reference from others purely for purposes of subtraction. Words, too, take more space than page numbers, although their significance in an index is actually less.

Another possible strategy for the avoidance of strings is the temptation to streamline falsely by converting an honest 8, 9, 10, 11, 12, 13, 14 to an apparently more acceptable 8–14. Neater, but less accurate. Despite appearances, a mere SMITH 30–48 indicates a lengthier, more sustained treatment of Smith in the text than does the more extensive index entry, SMITH 30, 33–4, 37, 39, 40–2, 45, 47–8.

In a long entry with many subheadings, where the arrangement is chronological, page references not deemed worthy of subheadings might be tucked into brackets in correct chronological place between page references with subheadings, thus:

> leaves school 45–8; (52, 55, 58); meets Joyce 63–6; (69, 72, 78); wedding 90–3; honeymoon 96–8; (100, 105, 109); moves to Suffolk 115–16; (123, 129, 136); applies for teaching post 140; ...

This has the advantage both of breaking up the string into shorter snippets, and letting these convey some information by their placing in sequence.

I would prefer to leave the lines of undifferentiated page numbers. The obvious message of an index entry is, 'information on this topic can be found on this page'. A rider may be, 'It has a subheading, taking up the space of several page numbers, so it must be important – well worth turning to'. A string of undifferentiated entries (in a conscientiously compiled index, that is) should bear its own, honest message: 'These are all minor references to this person/topic, none of which is worth emphasizing with a subheading' – especially if there are indeed some subheadings beneath the block of unadorned page numbers, indicating the difference in significance. (In a non-conscientiously compiled index, of course, such a block might show only that the indexer had been lazy, or starved of space, or relied on a computer flagging terms to merge references automatically and left it at that.)

We must recognize that a grade of references does exist between deserving omission and a subheading, and it causes necessary strings. There will be chronic cases of recurrent, trivial appearances: life's like that. There may even be virtue in a massive, undifferentiated block of page numbers. Collocation of dispersed references is achieved; and in one index, listing all references to the hero's drinking bouts, I saw no need to subdivide or more closely specify these – the simple agglomeration told its own startling tale, giving the answer not to, 'where, exactly?' but to, 'how much?'. Sub-strings – threads, perhaps – may occur when one subheading exactly fits a whole sequence of references: human lives may be repetitive businesses.

Strings of undifferentiated page references may indicate deliberate value judgement on the part of the indexer. I have described (page 54) a diary so rife with vituperative attack that I chose to give paragraphs merely of page numbers for these, not dignifying or endorsing them with summaries.

Literary language may present many slight references to a theme, separated in the text, but the repetition itself constituting significance. *Echoing* is a literary technique whereby a theme is never boldly stated, but hinted at so frequently that the effect is cumulative. In the novel *Possession* (Byatt, 1990), '[r]iddles and riddling', and snakes and serpents, are examples of this; lists could be compiled of the pages where they appear – or are hinted at, implied – but it would be clumsily overdoing it to clamp subheadings over the faint invocations. Strings of page numbers, undifferentiated, are just what would be needed here.

Strings have long had their distinguished advocates. James Thornton wrote of his index to Dickens' letters, which was to win the Wheatley Medal in 1969:

> What was wanted was a break-down of the material under broad heads. The index sins again and again against the rule that there should not be more than four or five undifferentiated references. To have introduced a great deal more descriptive matter simply out of regard for this rule would often have given a significance which was not born out by the text nor justified by anticipation of the interests of future readers. It would also frequently have meant that readers would find little more in the text than they already knew from the index. To make reference to the text is often for me an ideal of indexing, but to have followed this ideal with Dickens would have made the index unbearably long and confusing, with sub-classification carried to the fourth or fifth degree. (1965)

John Shaftesley, reviewing R. F. Hunnisett's *Indexing for editors* in 1972 proclaimed:

> Dr Hunnisett is on the side of those many indexers who believe it to be bad practice to have solid blocks of page numbers, unbroken by modifications, following particular entries. At the risk of a charge of philistinism, I do not wholeheartedly concur in this. If it is a question merely of aesthetics (which are important,

of course, even in the layout of lists), then I believe aesthetics are really not the criterion in the appearance of an index. If it is a question of adequacy, one must remind indexers that very often stern economics – not necessarily publishers' parsimony – may dictate the amount and cost of space to be devoted to it. Nor can every person, place, or subject, however numerous the page numbers their mention may demand, be supplied with enough important subheadings to justify separate treatment, yet the researcher needs every relevant page number that can be discovered. An index can look beautiful typographically, but it is essentially a working tool and one should not officiously strain to turn it into a master work of art visually. As Dr Hunnisett observes in another connection, an index entry is 'not a potted biography', and page numbers, when all is said and done, are its *raison d'être*.

In 2012 Christopher Phipps added his voice to the chorus, writing:

What is more problematic for the indexer [of a biographical text] is the walk-on player who makes multiple appearances, none of which is of notably significant importance. In other types of indexing, such references may rightly be judged as 'passing mentions' and therefore omitted from the index. But here [making an index entry for Dr Johnson's near-contemporary Edmund Burke in a biography of Johnson] I think such an approach would not be serving the index user well [...] I therefore opted (say it quietly) to include a simple string of locators [...] I would argue, an undifferentiated string of locators can be an eloquent indicator to the index user of the importance of the character in the narrative and the extent of the information they will find at any of the references.

Marian Aird, in 2016, pleaded the case for strings in indexes to volumes of letters:

the inclusion of casual but regular references to an individual, even when it is almost impossible to provide subheadings, is essential if the index is to be comprehensive [...] the long string of page numbers is as much evidence of [Britten's sister's] strong presence in his life as it is to any significant information about her in the text.

That ties up the matter nicely, we think.

An article about *strings* in *The Indexer* is:

The Ah!-factor. Hazel K. Bell. **17**(3), 191–2

---

12.   Presentation and layout

Prefatory notes

Major, massive, even whole-volume indexes need their individual plan and principles explained. Nearly forty entries concerning Pepys himself are listed after the preface to the volume-index to the diary. Knight (1970) observed of Thornton's index to Dickens' letters:

> Jame's Thorton's zeal for perfection is exemplified by his devoting a full page to the preliminary notes in which he explains: what names are, and what are not, included; how the names of title holders and married women will be found indexed, also localities, buildings and streets; that books and writings are entered mainly under the name of the author; and the meanings of the abbreviations and symbols employed.

The single-volume biography of Canning has a prefatory note of four paragraphs and a list: 'The following are among the more important abstract headings'. Forty are given, from ACTS OF INDIAN GOVT. to WHITE MUTINY (Macmillan, 1962).

Any abbreviations used in the index should be explained in a note at the head (as, 'RB in the index stands for Richard Burton; ET for Elizabeth Taylor'), and any departure from normal practice, as perhaps in the principle of indexing the peerage. It might also be stated if, for instance, page references in italics refer to illustrations and bold to major references, and whether the names of authors' works are dispersed through the index or gathered under their names. Readers of biographies, who are likely to be private individuals rather than information science bodies, may well be unaware that there are different systems of alphabetization, or standards for indexing, and I see no need to use space informing them of these. They are not given to studying notes before consulting indexes; more likely to plunge in and search around where they think entries are likely to be found than to devise a search path after consulting a long note.

Knight's index to Churchill 'begins with a note on its scope and on the meaning of the abbreviations and conventions used in it. This is a model of such a note, short but clear and exhaustive', wrote Richard Bancroft (Bancroft, 1968). The first two paragraphs of the prefatory note to the index of *Anthony Eden* are quoted on pages 37 and 69; the third adds, 'The abbreviation "AE" is used for Anthony Eden and "E" for Eden'. The whole note takes twelve lines, full across the page.

Run-on style

Chronological arrangement of subheadings with a narrative form seems to me to entail setting run-on, to reinforce the narrative reading effect. Indented style is best suited to alphabetical order, where the first letter of subheadings should be conspicuous, and the keywords brought to the front. Indented subheadings in narrative form are inappropriate, and give a staccato, disjointed effect; narrative requires the continuity of *sequence* of headings, which also allows retaining prepositions, whose use in indented subheadings is often deprecated. Scanning entries for unknown terms is easier when looking at dense blocks of print than following long, thin columns extending over pages.

In Wittmann's 1990 study of subheadings, 'All eight indexes had run-on subheadings, since a preliminary comparison of award-winning indexes suggested that run-on subheadings and set-out subheadings have characteristically different length and syntax'. Knight (1979) wrote that run-on sets of subheadings extending to several columns:

> not only produce a distasteful appearance but [are] wholly inimical to any ease of reference. I therefore take any credit that may be due for having devised the splitting up of any long list of subheadings into paragraphs [...] start a new paragraph after about every sixth subheading. If possible, each paragraph should open with a subheading of some significance. If the subheadings are arranged alphabetically, it may be neat and

convenient to begin each letter of the alphabet with a new paragraph.

This suggested paragraphing of Knight's is for visual relief only, not the meaningful division into headed paragraph sections used in the indexes to Dickens, Eden and Pepys, for example. Knight's entries are broken into paragraphs with no change to the order of headings, the breaks being unrelated to the meaning ('a new paragraph after about every sixth subheading'); and does not give the advantage of allowing another level of sub-subheadings within the paragraphs by section heads.

Within the paragraphs, set run-on, narrative subheadings may be read as chronological narrative, continuously. The ending of a subheading then may not necessarily discontinue its significance. For instance 'Marcus: living with Stephanie 50–60; after Mrs Orton arrives 70–80' in my index to Byatt's *Still life* does not have to imply that Marcus is no longer living with Stephanie after Mrs Orton's arrival. A subheading format to make this logically clear would be inappropriate – even clumsy – for a narrative index.

Sub-subheadings

Sub-subheadings are sometimes regarded as difficult to use in run-on layout. There are several possible methods of achieving this.

(1) Breaking the entry into paragraphs with section headings allows sub-subs of the main heading to become simple subheadings within each paragraph, giving another layer to play with.

(2) Subheading terms may also be repeated with each sub-sub, to form each time a new, complete subheading, as, e.g.:

> Brown, John: at school, friends; at school, prizes; at school, uniform

(3) The use of *brackets* allows a third layer of heading, as in:

> Abbey Theatre; [...] SO'C's relationship with, [...], (deterioration); *The Plough and the Stars* (submitted), (production), (programme), (controversy following); tours, [...]

Indented style

Sometimes indented style is used in a chiefly run-on-set index for particularly apposite selected paragraphs. In Matthews's index to Dickens, as described above, those paragraphs under the main heading that were arranged alphabetically were set in this way, among others set run-on. With alphabetical arrangement, the first word of each subheading needs to be clearly distinguishable, as, under DICKENS, CHARLES:

CHARACTERISTICS
abstemiousness
anger and temper
anxieties and fears
appearance and dress [...]; *see also* beard, below, *and*
    sub-heading Portraits
authoritarianism
beard and moustache

Ian Craine (2018) advocates a mixture of styles:

All biographies I've ever done demanded that the [main] subject was indexed. But you [...] need to find categories for collections of entries. I'd enter the first tier of subheadings in set-out – maybe a mix of chronological and alphabetical and quite possibly in upper case. So something like EARLY YEARS: EDUCATION: FIRST STEPS TO FAME: MARRIAGES: FRIENDS: PUBLICATIONS: OPINIONS OF OTHERS: OTHERS' OPINIONS OF etc. Then I'd do the second tier in run-on.

Typographical devices

Knight writes in 1966 of his use of typographical differentiation:

In the Churchill index, I have pulled out nearly every stop available to the indexer, including the open diapason of using bold type for page references for items to which more than a few lines are devoted in the text. Similarly I put page references in italics to denote illustrations or maps. I also use *bis* and (more occasionally) *ter* after a page reference to indicate that the subject is referred to quite separately twice or thrice respectively on the same page.

Two of the whole-volume biographical indexes considered here, those to Boswell and Pepys, resort in their indexes to special typographical conventions for differentiation. In 1967, de Beer wrote of Dr Powell's typographical usage (and of that of his predecessor in the indexing of Boswell, George Birkbeck Hill, in the Clarendon Press, six-volume edition of 1887):

> Both use heavy type for important keywords; Dr Powell to great advantage in entries such as those for Smollett and Virgil, where sub-entries for quotations must be distinguished from the rest. Where Dr Powell excels is in the typography of the longer complex entries, and especially in some of those that are divided into numerical sections:
>
> > To facilitate consultation of the very long articles on the major characters, letters, corresponding to the initials of the keywords of the entries, are inserted in their appropriate places; these, and the important keywords themselves, are printed in heavy type, e.g. BOSWELL: **A** account of himself; **B** enters at the bar; **C** visits Cambridge; **D** buys Dalblair; **drinking**: a lover of wine. [...] Italics are used in headings and subheadings for titles of books and plays, and for ships' names; and for words discussed by Johnson. The last is important.

This last usage also indicates how indexers may resort to special devices in order to cope with the particular contents of each text for indexing, rather than look to standard precepts to cover all contingencies.

Robert Latham evolved a whole complicated stratification to cope with Samuel Pepys himself in the index to the diary. An article on the design of indexes approved the result: 'This example shows how complex entries can be presented well for the reader's use; a variety of distinction of elements has been used' (Ridehalgh, 1985).

Latham (1984) explains:

[Pepys] had to be dealt with for the most part under a series of distinct headings – HEALTH, DIARY (P), CLERK OF THE ACTS, BOOKS, MUSIC and so on.

The principal entries concerning Pepys are listed on the page following the preface to the index volume. There are nearly forty of these, including four under *General*: Pepys, Samuel, recollections of early life; Correspondence; Diary (P); Writings; 12 under *Career*, nine under *Private Life*, and 13 under *Interests and tastes*.

Bernard Levin (1983) described this index as:

a huge compilation; 600 columns [...] not merely exhaustive but exhaustively detailed. I have tried every kind of trick question I could think of on this astonishing guide to the Diary, and have not been able to catch it out in a single *lacuna*.

He gives details of the 'very substantial' entry for HEALTH:

The entry is divided into 'Health (illness/disease/condition)' and 'Health (remedies/treatment)'. The first of these is divided into 51 sub-sections headed in small capitals ('ABSCESS, AGUE, ALLERGY, APOPLEXY, [...] TOOTHACHE, ULCER, VOMITING') and each of these contains up to 30 topical headings; the second is split still further, remedies and treatment being divided into 'MEDICINAL' ('BALSAM, CORDIAL, DIURETIC ...'), 'SURGICAL' ('AMPUTATIONS, CAUTERY, DENTISTRY ...'), 'DRESSINGS', 'DIET', and 'OTHER TREATMENTS', each of these sub-subheadings being in turn further broken down topically.

To illustrate the use of varying typefaces, indentations, and new lines for major subheadings in this index, we quote part of an entry just as it is set out in the original volume, with facsimile line breaks. Note that full capitals are used for main headings, with turnovers indented one character; small caps for subheadings, not indented; small caps also for sub-subs, indented two characters, with text then run-on, turnovers indented only one character.

DRESS AND PERSONAL APPEAR-
ANCE (MEN AND BOYS) {*see also*
Prices; Watches etc.}:
GENERAL (P): importance of good
linen, 3/216, 228; 8/121; and neatness,
2/199 & n. 1; to dress fashionably,
4/343, 357; 5/269, 302; 6/100;
concerned at expense, 2/47, 129;
4/356, 357; 6/104; concerned not to
overdress, 9/551
GARMENTS AND ACCESSORIES:
APRONS: worn by apprentice
weavers, 5/222
BANDS: King's lack of, 8/417; (P):
1/85, ... 7/61; lace/fine bands, 3/215, ...
in plain band mistaken for servant,
8/115; band strings, 2/80
BELTS (P): sword belt, 4/80;
7/26, [...] 537
BOOTS (P): ridingboots, 1/279;
2/132; ...
BREECHES: two legs through one
knee of, 2/66 & n.2; (P): baize
linings, 1/268; closeknee'd, 3/106;
white linings, 4/130; rabbit skin
prevents galling, 5/298; silk, 6/218;
camlet, 9/533

Typographical distinction fails in the index to Spalding's *Vanessa Bell*. The paragraph headings for the main character's entry are each set at the beginning of a line, but in italics, similarly to the titles of works of art and literature. They are thus visually indistinguishable from titles, and those titles (or parts of titles) that appear at the beginnings of lines could be taken as subheads. Some such strange simulated subheads in this index entry appear to be: RMS Queen Mary; Fry; Poppies; Nursery Tea; Kitchen.

However, for most of us, engaged in the day-to-day indexing of biographies of *c.*300 pages, just a few of these conventions are likely to prove sufficient: **bold type** for major references among a sequence of minor ones; SMALL CAPITALS for paragraph headings; *italics* for book and journal titles, and for the equivalent of stage directions – those terms not actually part of the index but outside, administering it: *see, see also titles of books*.

Piggott gives warning against overdoing it, citing *Recherches sur les Confessions de Saint Augustin* by Pierre Courcelle (Boccard, 1950) (Piggott, 1991):

> Typography does all the work of subheadings in the general index. Bold type is used for names of persons closely connected with Augustine until his 35th year; small capitals for names of other persons in antiquity; italics for words and expressions with historical, doctrinal or philological interest; and ordinary roman for the rest. So one finds:

> **Ambroise de Milan** [and his page reference in bold]
> ANNIBAL [in small capitals]
> Carthage [in roman]
> *démons* [in italic]
> *figuier symbolique* [in italic]
> Harris [a modern writer quoted, in roman]

It is ingenious, repulsive to look at, and, surely, not very helpful.

Michael Brackney had some most intriguing ideas for typographical distinctions of index items. For instance, when general descriptions and mere mentions are referenced together directly after the main headings, to make clear which are which, he suggests indexing general discussions with locators underlined, 'which would serve as an unobtrusive indication of importance similar to the indication of importance supplied by a subheading'; and indexing passing mentions with locators formatted in gray (the opposite of bold type for major references) – or in superscript numerals. He suggests combining two same-page locators such as 61, *61* (or *61*, 61), that indicate text and illustration occurring on the same page, into a single locator, as in 61* or *61** (or even *61*≡, using an icon to represent lines of text), and as in

61+*ph*. As to *passim* ... he considered using a tilde or ellipsis points as a page range concatenator, turning a conventional page range into the typographic equivalent of *passim*. But, 'although [he] liked the discrete spaciousness of the ellipsis points, [he] found their implication of "something left out" to be too antithetical to the meaning of *passim.*' Instead he advocates three hyphens, as in 44---50, or three raised dots, as in 44···50, 'as a symbolic equivalent of *passim* – a veritable graphic representation of discrete passages that is compact in proportional fonts' (Bell, 2008a).

In 2011 Brackney won the Wilson Award for Excellence in Indexing for his index to *Dogen's Extensive Record: A Translation of the Eihei Koroku* – a translation of a collection of works by a Sōtō Zen monk – published by Wisdom Publications. In this index Brackney used some of his own typographical distinctions, explained in the headnote thus:

- Bold page numbers indicate either primary references to persons or actual pages of Dogen's text.

- Page numbers followed by (2) indicate two separate discussions.

- Page numbers followed by q indicate quotations.

- Page numbers followed by n plus a number, as in 75n1, indicate footnotes.

- Page numbers followed by +n plus a number, as in 75+n2, indicate discussions plus footnotes.

- Page numbers followed by t indicate tables.

A splendid array indeed! And an ideal for indexers to aspire to?

Articles on the **design and layout of indexes** that have appeared in *The Indexer* are:

The typography of indexes. S. I. Wicklen. **1**(1), 36–41
The typography of indexes. Robin Kinross. **10**(4), 179–85
Printer and indexer. Hugh Williamson. **12**(2), 65–72

The design of indexes. Nan Ridehalgh. **14**(3), 165–74
How the publishers want it to look. Jean Simpkins. **17**(1), 41–2
The visual appeal of indexes: an exploration. Frances S. Lennie. **28**(2), 60–7
The Chicago manual of style on indexes: how it has changed. Sylvia Coates. **36**(2), 68–70

13.   The user

Who are the users of our indexes? Ian Craine (2018) claims:

> I believe an index is for future readers, not publishers, not authors, not the Society of Indexers training manuals, not Quality Standards.

There are various particular groups of likely readers of biographies and users of their indexes, with varying specific requirements. Genealogists and researchers of family histories search eagerly for the smallest reference to a name, trivial though the mention may be in the book. A historian speaking at a conference of the Society of Indexers begged us to include in our indexes the names of all people mentioned, down to the most minor references to servants in the background, to help researchers such as herself (Bell, 1996).

Another group of users – reviewers – are reputed sometimes to look only at the index of a book, hoping to find there sufficient summary of the text and indication of its chief topics to spare them the reading. As mentioned earlier (page 7), this is blandly acknowledged by Whittemore (1999), who writes: 'For an ordinary newspaper reviewer, for instance [...] a biography should have a good index to help him skip perhaps half a thousand pages.'

Students, too, may see indexes as short-cuts to knowledge. Anita Heiss confessed that she 'managed to get through some subjects in [her] undergraduate degree by only reading indexes of books' (Heiss, 2015). Paul Gifford, reviewing Michel Jarrety's *Paul Valèry*, referred to the 'serviceable index (helpful to the far greater number who will consult it as a reference book)' (Gifford, 2009).

Is that me ...?

'Most biographies are about dead people,' Alain de Botton observes (1995). But the readership of current biographies and autobiographies may well include living characters featured in the text, and therefore also in the index – indexees, we may call them. Some may yearn to appear there: one confessed, 'Shamefully I admit to having bought one or two books simply on the strength of having seen my name in the index [...] It seems some men count their index mentions as others count sexual conquests' (Roy, 1993). Michael Lister, reviewing Frederic Raphael's autobiography, *Cuts and bruises* (Carcanet, 2006), accuses the author, assumed also to be the book's indexer, of:

> provid[ing] a name index [...] to satisfy those, about whom the author has written elsewhere,'who look first in the index of their contemporaries' books to see if they are cited. It is better to be abused than ignored'. (Lister, 2006)

Andy McSmith attributed the same considerate motive to Tam Dalyell, in reviewing his memoir, *The importance of being awkward* (Birlinn, 2011). He wrote:

> He has an absurdly polite habit of name-checking everyone he has known whom he thinks deserves to be remembered. By my approximate count, over 600 of his contemporaries are listed in the index. (McSmith, 2011)

The most sensitive of potential indexees are likely to be politicians. The'Washington read', defined as: 'the perusal of a book by checking the index for references, usually to oneself, and reading only those parts of the book' (Lee, 2004) was described in Chapter 1, relating to political memoirs. Campbell (2008) wrote:

> The only thing worse for a politician than a morning newspaper without his name in it is a political book without his name in it [...]. Books hang around, and if you're not mentioned they just sit there as constant reminders of your insignificance. When a new political book comes out, MPs hit the bookstores – always at odd hours, to avoid detection – and discreetly examine the

index to see if they are mentioned. If not, the book is banned from the MP's office. If you are mentioned, you buy multiple copies for friends and family. (Note to publishers: to increase sales, pack your indexes with as many politicos as possible.)

Assuredly, however trivial the reference in the text, such characters would wish to be included in the index.

Indexees may even be appointed reviewers of the books in which they appear. Thus, Victoria Glendinning, reviewing *Martha Gellhorn: a life* by Caroline Moorehead (Chatto, 2003), frankly declared, 'I am not without bias. I know the author of this biography. My name is in the index. This is the kind of thing that gives book reviewing a bad name' (Glendinning, 2003). While Germaine Greer, on receipt of a review copy, stormed: 'There's no way I could avoid being sent a complimentary copy of Tony Moore's *Dancing with empty pockets: Australia's bohemians*. I have no intention whatever of reading it, if only because my name is a bulky entry in the index' (Greer, 2012).

Articles on the **user** that have appeared in *The Indexer* are:

Indexes for local and family history: a user's view. John Chandler. **13**(4), 223–7

User approaches to indexes [family history]. Jean Stirk. **16**(2), 75–8

Whom should we aim to please? Hazel K. Bell. **20**(1), 3–5

Information access or information anxiety? An exploratory evaluation of book index features. Elizabeth D. Liddy and Corinne L. Jörgensen. **20**(2), 64–8

Let's get usable! Usability studies for indexes. Susan C. Olason. **22**(2), 91–5

Who are we indexing for exactly? Michèle Clarke. **26**(1), 35

---

14.   Fiction

Indexers are unlikely to be commissioned to index works of fiction, other than (and that rarely) cumulative indexes to sets of works. However, the indexing of fiction – which certainly consists of soft, narrative texts – is an interesting topic deserving of consideration here.

Should fiction be indexed?

Although by no means standard practice, the indexing of fiction has been undertaken from time to time. Serious novels may be indexed in the same way as biographies or histories, as narratives concerning groups of people and the events in their lives. Indexes to fiction may be needed more now that chapter synopses no longer appear in contents lists.

Some of the authors consulted by Philip Bradley in a survey of views as to the need for indexes to fiction objected to the idea of fiction being indexed, holding that it might destroy the magic, 'positively detrimental to the aims of fiction as an imaginative, creative genre' (Bradley, 1989). Indexers too have expressed reservations. Douglas Matthews opposes the indexing of fiction:

> This kind of analysis of creative writing (whether fiction, poetry or drama), which is form, rather than of, say, biography which is documentation, presumes a reality which is not there. Conventionally, an index is concerned with facts. The index you construct is itself a fiction. [...] Teasing out entries from the text is damaging rather than enhancing, like pulling out the threads from a patterned carpet to see what makes the design. (personal communication, 1990)

Indexing biographies

David Wilson considers:

> Perhaps the hankering for indexes to novels (insofar as it exists at all) is sheer laziness. If we feel we need an index to Proust, or Dickens, say, this is only because we haven't been reading with sufficient concentration. Dickens did give a helping hand to his readers, in the early novels at least. It's easier to find a particular passage in *Pickwick* than in *Our mutual friend*, and the chapter-rubrics of Fielding and Smollett are as entertaining as most modern novels, and far fuller of incident. The only novel I hold genuinely unnavigable without an index is *Finnegans wake*. (personal communication, 1988)

But if indexes are to be held suitable adjuncts to any texts, to allow the location of specific passages and collate dispersed references to the same theme, then surely fiction that is serious, lengthy, and complex is at least as deserving of these aids to study and research as any other form of writing. Serious fiction combines elements of direct conveying of information, as employed in histories, in its plots and their developments, with literary style which deploys language with subtlety, imagination, association, implication, and individual response – the unindexable elements. Indexing could spare the symbolism, the metaphors and the magic, restricting its work to names, places and recorded events.

Andrew Ellis positively craved such indexes, writing in 1992:

> How often I have wished that certain categories of fiction, to which I return frequently, were indexed – for instance, certain *oeuvres* such as the novels of L. P. Hartley – and novel 'series' or 'sequences' like the Barsetshire novels of Angela Thirkell.

Anthony Raven argued on this issue:

> The facts in a work of fiction may have no independent existence outside it, whereas those in a work of non-fiction do exist independently of the book, but that is irrelevant. Within the context of the book, which is all an index is concerned with, the one kind of fact is every bit as factual, and as indexable, as the

other. [...] within the context of a book, i.e. within the purview of its index, all facts are equally factual, regardless of whether they also enjoy a different kind of factuality beyond the book's covers. [...] book indexes index books, not real life. (Raven, 1990)

F. W. Lancaster considers the indexing and abstracting of fiction, suggesting that '[t]he indexing of imaginative works is likely to be more subjective and interpretative than other types', and complicated further by their essentially open-ended scope. 'Since the context of imaginative works is not restricted by subject matter, subject expertise, in the conventional sense, is irrelevant to the situation.' He concludes, 'It is likely that imaginative works present greater difficulties for the indexer than other types of publication' (Lancaster, 1991).

Simon Stern gives detailed examination of sixteenth–seventeenth century indexes to literature – novels and poetry (Stern, 2009). He writes that at first they served merely as memory prompts, plot summaries, but came to 'provide information of a different order', such as moral reflections; and later also to 'pique the reader's curiosity', adding value to the book as an enticement. Some more detailed indexes with long entries guided readers to the treatment of some issue on which the book might provide a useful maxim. Stern finds that indexes of that period often took an 'oddly jumbled form – mixing plot summaries, apothegms, and cryptic summaries of their moral assessments'.

The indexer as literary critic

The indexing of fiction to some extent occurs in the valid indexing of literary criticism. Take for example these entries from the index to Charles Dickens' *Great expectations* in the series of Icon Critical Guides (Tredell, 1998):

> Estella: and Biddy; characterisation; cruelty; and Miss Havisham; Magwitch as father; murderess for mother; and Pip
> food: Magwitch in churchyard; Magwitch in London; Pip at Satis House
> hands: Estella's; Jaggers's; Pip-Magwitch; ritual

> Havisham, Miss: and Compeyson; as death; desire; eccentricity; and Estella; hanging hallucination; madness; mothering; and Pip; traits

As observed regarding reading the text (page 29), Tom Murphy explored 'the possibilities of indexing as a teaching tool' for studying literature, as such indexing 'required a special kind of close reading – one that could not rest on merely superficial understandings but demanded a recursive flow, the constant back and forth of careful reading and re-reading' (Murphy, 2003).

Robert Irwin's satirical article, 'Your novel needs indexing' (Irwin, 2000), was reviewed in the *TLS* as:

> a study in tongue-in-cheek academicism, purporting to examine the indexing of novels as 'a transgressive act [...] something that can provide the work of fiction with an additional metatextual level'. Irwin provides examples of how an index can warn that a book is not worth reading, give you a fast forward on one character's love life, or indicate the lunacy of the author.
>
> Indeed, he observes 'what a useful critical tool a carefully-assembled index can be'. (Halliburton, 2000)

Robert Collison (1962) too felt that he had turned literary critic in indexing the novels of Robert Smith Surtees, writing:

> The indexer, as no-one else, sees the author at his desk and waits with eagerness to see whether he will take this opportunity or avoid that trap. Often there is the temptation to cry out 'what a chance to develop the plot was missed here', and often there is a regret that some insignificant character was left unexploited and featureless. Even the literary critic does not achieve the remorseless degree of criticism to which the indexer is impelled by the very nature of his work [...]. Once the first shock of seeing the inner workings is over, a new and deeper interest develops which leads to a far readier appreciation of an author's work.

Douglas Matthews wrote in 2004 of Pickering and Chatto's project 'to republish a large part of the Defoe canon [...] 44 volumes, grouped under five thematic headings: [...] [the last being] The Novels (10)'. He was commissioned to index 'Defoe's works as they appeared' (Matthews, 2004). However, when Volume 10 of THE NOVELS OF DANIEL DEFOE was published in 2009, it was headed:

CONSOLIDATED INDEX
This index covers the introductions and explanatory notes only.

– a great disappointment to some.

The index, compiled by the author, to Philip Hensher's novel *The fit* (Fourth Estate, 2004), extends and illustrates the theme of the text. The protagonist and narrator of the book is himself an indexer. John Sutherland (2006) points out:

> the rape and murder of his sister, Frankie, 17 years earlier [...] is that event from which John's life has become a neurotic, never-ending, tormented flight. 'Frankie', significantly, has no entry in the index. Indexing is a means of rendering her invisible.

In a chapter on narratives in *Writing lives: principia biographica*, Leon Edel treats Virginia Woolf's *Orlando* at length as a unique case to study the relationship of fiction to biography, calling it 'a fantasy in the form of a biography' (Edel, 1984):

> In keeping with its nature the volume is endowed with an index. The pretence of scholarship and exactitude is maintained to the end. Yet it is a rather mischievous index, for it supplies data not in the text [...]. Such then are the conventional trappings which dress out this fantasy-biography.

Gustave Flaubert claimed that his only true biography took the form of his novel, *Madame Bovary* (Holmes, 1997).

The question is often argued of whether typographical distinction should be made between 'real' characters in fiction (i.e. those with historical life in the real world) and those of the authors' imagination. I would suggest not; although, for example, the Duke and Duchess of Windsor undoubtedly have historical reality, their actions as depicted in William Boyd's novel *Any human heart* (Hamish Hamilton, 2002) are fictitious, and should not be accorded apparent historical authentication by use of a specified 'reality-indicating' typeface.

Indexes to fiction could be particularly valuable for sequences of novels, such as Galsworthy's *Forsyte Saga* or A. N. Wilson's *The Lampert Papers*, or for those of authors who replay the same characters in separate novels – such as Alison Lurie, with her frequently recurring members of the ramifying Stockwell and Zimmern families, so fascinating to recognize on unsignalled reappearance in a new context.

Indexing the fiction of A. S. Byatt

Bradley, indexing Walter Scott's Waverley novels, found the problems of indexing fiction to arise chiefly from lack of standardization of page numbers, chapter numbering, spelling and nomenclature in different editions of the same works (Bradley, 1989). In indexing five novels by A. S. Byatt (Byatt, 1978, 1986, 1990) I found more abstract coils of difficulty in indexing fictional rather than historic lives (Bell, 1991).

Fictional works contain much more than mere information, the usual quarry of indexers. The text of novels is more complex than that of biography because of the amount going on in each scene; as well as basic plot development (corresponding to the development of the career of the main character in a biography), there were in the Byatt novels always developing relationships, images, symbols, themes, with their significance to be interpreted and a suitable means of recording them devised. It was often difficult to devise a single subheading to cover even one paragraph for one character in the Byatt novels: to select one aspect as the term of the subheading might be to dismiss several other possible ones.

Indexers are supposed to select only 'significant' items from the text for listing in the index. How to determine significance, in such rich, detailed, widely allusive writing, is perplexing indeed. The subtlety and complexity of the literary form make it particularly difficult to devise headings that fully convey 'aspect' – what is said – rather than mere 'aboutness' – what is referred to – as differentiated by Weinberg (1988). The significance of the text may simply overload the index term, not to be conveyed in the index. Byatt's themes were abstract and complex, and quite differently treated among different characters and scenes of the novels. How far to index symbols and metaphors became a most delicate question.

Characters in fiction are presented and interpreted in various ways and at many levels. Biographers and historians rarely give long thought sequences, or detailed dreams, of their subjects, but these occur often in fiction; historians know less of their characters, and tell us less, than the authors of fiction, who, creating their own characters and so possessing total knowledge of them, can fully present both their inner and outer lives. Fiction may present its events also as recounted in characters' conversations. Should one enter for a person only references to their actual appearances and actions in the novel, or also treat as valid references mentions of them in the conversations, dreams or thoughts of others? So much that happens in the Byatt novels is implicit only, or comprehensible only in the light of later developments, that for some entries bald assumptions must be made. Literary language has been called 'a language of evocation, not of reference' (Cioffi, 1998). The structure of the whole, and the unity of each chapter of these novels, have been deliberately engineered by a literary writer in a way that the factual recording of historic events does not need to be.

Problems of the devising and arrangement of subheadings for the several major characters in fiction are more complex than those encountered in biographies. The narrative is not always simply chronological. Flashbacks are a frequent form; memories and thoughts of characters play a large part. Two periods may be simultaneously presented: the time when someone is engaged in reflection, and the time they are remembering.

For my index to Byatt's novel, *Still life*, I needed subheadings I had never used before – 'conception' as the first chronological entry for two of the children, clearly designated. Babies were important in the stories, needing new subheadings for babyhood. All human life was here indeed.

Novels published with indexes

Fiction and indexes, the pamphlet published by the Society of Indexers (2nd edition, 2002) includes an annotated list of novels by 37 different authors published with indexes (I have been able to name only two of the indexers). Not all of them, by any means, are properly serious, full indexes, however.

Indexing biographies

Some of those indexes are limited to listing names only: e.g. *Emma* and *Pride and prejudice* by Jane Austen, in editions by R. W. Chapman (Oxford University Press, 1923); Olivia Goldsmith, *Bestseller* (HarperCollins, 1996); Kurt Vonnegut, *Jailbird* (Cape, 1979). The index to J. R. R. Tolkien's *Silmarillion* (Allen & Unwin, 1977) is to names only, but provided with full glosses. Others list only other particular types of item: 'Moral and Instructive Sentiments, Maxims, Cautions and Reflexions' in Samuel Richardson's own index to his novels, *Clarissa* (3rd ed., 1751) and *Sir Charles Grandison* (1754); only philosophers and philosophical concepts in Jostein Gaarder's *Sophie's world: a novel about the history of philosophy* (Phoenix House, 1995); only mythological characters in John Updike's *The centaur* (Deutsch, 1963). Wilton Barnhardt's *Gospel* (St Martin's Press, 1993) is fiction, but includes historical personages and events; only these 'purely factual matters' are indexed.

Larger works – sequences of novels – may have a series of indexes of separate categories. Honoré de Balzac's *La comédie humaine* (Garnier-Flammarion, 1976–81) has an index of 775 pages in four parts: *Index des personnages fictifs; Index des personnes réelles et des personnages historiques ou de la mythologie; Index des citées par Balzac; Index des oeuvres des personnages fictifs.* Marcel Proust's *A la recherche du temps perdu* (Pleiade edition, 1954) has an index of 151 pages in two parts: *Index des noms de personnes* and *Index alphabétique des noms de lieux, de contrées et d'habitants.* J. R. R. Tolkien's *The Lord of the rings* (HarperCollins, 2001) has a 24-page index, divided into four sections: Songs and verses; Persons, beasts and monsters; Places; Things.

Some novelists provide their own indexes purely for comedy, such as Lucy Ellmann, *Sweet desserts* (Virago, 1988); A. P. Herbert, *Bardot, M.P.? and other modern misleading cases,* (Methuen, 1964), *Misleading cases in the common law* (1929), *More misleading cases* (1930), and *Uncommon law* (1935); and Lemony Snicket, *Lemony Snicket: the unauthorized autobiography* (HarperCollins). Lewis Carroll provided 'an index whose whimsicality perfectly fitted the equally whimsical text' (Wellisch, 1992) to the first edition of *Sylvie and Bruno* (Macmillan 1889), and a combined index to both novels with *Sylvie and Bruno concluded* in 1893. Sadly, when the Sylvie and Bruno books have been reprinted in those one-volume tomes purporting to be 'The complete works of Lewis Carroll', the indexes to Sylvie and Bruno are regularly omitted (Imholtz, 1996).

Some authors add indexes to fictitious biographies to lend an air of authenticity: Ranulph Fiennes, in *The feather men* and *The sett* (Little Brown); Daniel Defoe, *Memoirs of a cavalier* (Oxford edition, 1972); George Gissing, *The private papers of Henry Ryecroft* (Archibald Constable, 1903; Bell, 2006a); and Virginia Woolf, *Orlando* (Hogarth Press, 1928: a basic, simple index: little over two pages to 215 pages of text). Fiennes' two books are described by the publishers as 'factional novels': the original, hardback editions ask 'Fact or fiction?' on the covers.

William Boyd's *Any human heart*, for example, is a fictional diary, 1923–91, purportedly kept by Logan Mountstuart, 490 pages, with footnotes, to which Boyd himself provided an 11-page index. Asked on the BookBrowse website why, he replied:

> The search for authenticity and plausibility: to encourage the reader's suspension of disbelief. To encounter an index at the end of a novel is extremely rare and somehow questions the novel's fictionality for a second or two. It was great fun to compile as well, you have in the index Logan's life in microcosm and it can almost be read independently: you'd get a sense of who Logan Mountstuart was and what his life contained.

Some of the indexes listed in the Society of Indexers' pamphlet seem quite surrealistic: Malcolm Bradbury, *My strange quest for Mensonge* (Deutsch, 1987); Mark Z. Danielewski, *House of leaves* (Anchor, 2000); Harry Mathews, *The sinking of the Odradek Stadium* (Carcanet, 1971–2); Milorad Pavic, *Landscape painted with tea* (Knopf, 1990); Georges Perec, *Life: a user's manual: fictions* (trans. David Bellos; Collins Harvill, 1988).

In fact, the only proper subject indexes to fiction listed in that brochure seem to be those to: Clive James, *Brilliant creatures* (Cape, 1983 – index by Ann Kingdom); Jerome K. Jerome, *Three men in a boat* (annotated edition; Pavilion Books / Michael Joseph, 1982 – index by Anthony Raven); and George Orwell, *Nineteen eighty-four* (OUP, Clarendon Press, 1984).

Many of these indexes to fiction, and others, were further considered in 'Fiction published with indexes in chronological order of publication' (Bell, 2007).

Since then, indexes have been included to add apparent veracity to fictional memoirs, as well as for comedy, in *Alan Partridge: nomad* by Steve Coogan et al. (Trape, 2016); *I, Partridge: we need to talk about Alan* by Steve Coogan et al. (HarperCollins, 2011); and *Toast on Toast: cautionary tales and candid advice* by M. Berry and A. Mathews (Canongate, 2015).

Among other more serious examples of fiction seeking to appear authentic by the provision of indexes are: Robert Sobel's *For want of a nail: if Burgoyne had won at Saratoga* (Greenhill Books, 1977), an 'alternative history' about the American Revolutionary War, provided with an authenticating 14-page index; *A strangeness in my mind* by Orhan Pamuk (Faber, 2015), a fictional family story set in Istanbul over 40+ years, its purported authenticity provided with a genealogical chart, chronology, and index; and Alain de Botton's *Kiss and tell* (Macmillan, 1995), a pseudobiography (246 pages) with a pseudobiographical, properly detailed and structured index (12 pages) complete with full breakdown into subheadings (provided also with 'family trees' and photographs).

The 1906 edition from Hutchinson & Co. of *The life and opinions of Tristram Shandy, Gentleman* by Laurence Sterne (640 pp) includes a nine-and-a-half page 'Index of Persons and Words' – highly, and illogically, selective (Phipps, 2006).

Other strange, partial indexes: Alasdair Gray's *Lanark* (Panther, 1982) includes in the margins of the epilogue 'An index of diffuse and imbedded plagiarisms'.

Invisible power: a philosophical adventure story by Philip Allot (Xlibris Corporation, 2005), after its 89-page narrative includes a page giving 'Instructions for the use of this book' which concludes 'Thereafter the reader may wish to read the Index where the contents of the book are presented in molecular form', and a 23-page single-column index with its own heading, 'Genome of a Human Reality: INDEX EXPLAINED: Using the generic genetic mental elements (GGME's) listed below, in different proportions and different arrangements, it would be possible to construct any number of alternative human realities (AHR's)' (Bell, 2006).

Fictitious works first published index-less to which indexes are later supplied (sometimes more than once) include, as well as those listed above: John Bunyan's *Pilgrim's progress, The life and death of Mr. Badman* and *The holy war*; Henry Fielding's *Amelia* and *Tom Jones*; and Walter Scott's *Waverley* novels.

Articles about indexing fiction, and examples of such indexes, are also to be found on the Internet, particularly on Tom Murphy's website: www.brtom.org/ind.html. His indexes to Fitzgerald's *The great Gatsby*, Tim O'Brien's *The things they carried* and John Gardner's *Grendel* are all accessible online, as are Suzanne Morine's index to Salinger's *The catcher in the rye*, Lisa Mirabile's to *The English patient* by Michael Ondaatje and my own to A. S. Byatt's *The virgin in the garden* and *Still life* (combined), *Babel tower* and *A whistling woman* (combined) and *Possession*; and cumulative indexes to the novels of J. L. Carr, Molly Keane, Iris Murdoch, Barbara Pym and Angela Thirkell.

Articles on the **indexing of fiction** that have appeared in *The Indexer* are:

A long fiction index [to Scott's Waverley novels]. Philip Bradley. **8**(3), 153–63

Para-index and anti-index (*Sweet Desserts*). Judy Batchelor. **16**(3), 194

Indexes to works of fiction: the views of producers and users on the need for them. Philip Bradley. **16**(4), 239–46

Indexes to works of fiction (letter). Anthony Raven. **17**(1), 60–1

Indexing fiction: a story of complexity. Hazel K. Bell. **17**(3), 51–6

Should fiction be indexed? The indexability of text. Hazel K. Bell. **18**(2), 83–6

A Marshland index – or 'Indexing for the Hell of it' (on his compilation of indexes to the fiction of S. L. Bensusan). John Vickers. **19**(4), 276–9

Indexer nascitur, non fit – Lewis Carroll as indexer again. August A. Imholtz, Jr. **20**(1), 11–13

Indexes as fiction and fiction as paper-chase [*War fever* and *Pale fire*]. Hazel K. Bell. **20**(4), 209–11

Thirty-nine to one: indexing the novels of Angela Thirkell. Hazel K. Bell. **21**(1), 6–10

Kiss and tell and index. Hazel K. Bell. **21**(4), 180–1

Exploring fiction and poetry through indexing. Tom Murphy. **23**(4), 216–17

Sterne stuff. Christopher Phipps. **25**(2), 112–13

Review, *The private papers of Henry Ryecroft.* Hazel K. Bell. **25**(2), 149–50

Review, *Invisible power.* Hazel K. Bell. **25**(2), 150–1

Fiction published with indexes: in chronological order of publication. Hazel K. Bell. **25**(3), 169–75

Fictional characters in non-fiction works. Madeleine Davis. **29**(2), 65–9

'As if we were reading a good novel': fiction and the index from Richardson to Ballard. Dennis Duncan. **32**(1), 2–11

Back of the book, back of the net: the comedy books indexes of Partridge and Toast. Paula Clarke Bain. **35**(1), 18–24

See also: 'Your novel needs indexing'. Robert Irwin, in *New writing 9* ed. A. L. Kennedy & John Fowles, Vintage 2000.

References

Abel, Richard (1991) 'Books that are not being written', *LOGOS* **2**(3), 164–7.
Abel, Richard (1993) 'Measuring the value of books', *LOGOS* **4**(1), 36–44.
Aird, Marian (2016) '"Your letters have been life and breath to me": the
   challenge of indexing *My beloved man*', *The Indexer* **34**(4), 138–43.
American Society for Indexing (n.d.) 'ASI excellence in indexing award',
   American Society for Indexing, https://www.asindexing.org/about/awards/
   asi-indexing-award/.
Anderson, Margaret D. (1962) 'An indexer appeals to authors', *The Indexer*
   3(1), Spring, 24.
Anderson, Margaret D. (1971) *Book indexing*. Cambridge University Press,
   p. 23.
Anderson, Marilyn (2002) American Society of Indexers website,
   www.indexing.org.
Asquith, Lady Cynthia (1968) *Diaries 1915–18*. Hutchinson, 1968.
Awards roundup (2017) *The Indexer* **35**(3), 126.
Awards roundup (2018) *The Indexer* **36**(3), 123.
Bancroft, Richard (1964) 'Some requirements of good indexes', *The Indexer*
   4(1), Spring, 19.
Bancroft, Richard (1968) 'The Wheatley Medal, 1967', *The Indexer* **6**(2),
   Autumn, 59–63.
Barlow, Caroline (1998) 'Counterblasts to professionalism – 2', *The Indexer*
   21(1), April, 40.
Barnes, Julian (2000) *Something to declare*. Picador, pp. 115, 195, 245.
Barnett, Paul (1983) 'Beyond the appendix with gun and camera', *The Indexer*
   13(4), October, 232–35.
Batchelor, Judy L. (1983) 'Indexing to please the eye', *The Indexer* **13**(4),
   October, 258.
Bell, Hazel K. (1990) 'Indexing biographies: the main character', *The Indexer*
   17(1), April, 43–4.
Bell, Hazel K. (1991a) 'The Ah!-factor', *The Indexer* **17**(3), April, 191–2.

Bell, Hazel K. (1991b) 'Indexing fiction: a story of complexity', *The Indexer* 17(4), October, 251–6.

Bell, Hazel K. (1996) 'Whom should we aim to please?', *The Indexer* 20(1), April, 3–5.

Bell, Hazel K. (2000) 'Open Letter to the Panel Judging the Wheatley Award', *Catalogue & Index* 135, 5; *SIdelights* (2), Summer, 12–13.

Bell, Hazel K. (2004) '"Discursive, dispersed, heterogeneous": indexing *Seven pillars of wisdom*', *The Indexer* 24(1), 9–11.

Bell, Hazel K. (2006a) Review, *The Indexer* 25(2), 149–50.

Bell, Hazel K. (2006b) Review, *The Indexer* 25(2), 150–1.

Bell, Hazel K. (2007) 'Fiction published with indexes in chronological order of publication', *The Indexer* 25(3), 169–75.

Bell, Hazel K. (2008a) 'Michael Brackney: thinking outside the box', in *From Flock Beds to Professionalism: a history of index-makers*. Oak Knoll Press, pp. 193–5.

Bell, Hazel K. (2008b) 'Laura Moss Gottlieb: indexing softly', in *From Flock Beds to Professionalism: a history of index-makers*. Oak Knoll Press, pp. 209–11.

Boswell, James (1887) *Life of Johnson*. Edited by George Birkbeck Hill. Clarendon Press.

Boswell, James (1934–64) *The Life of Samuel Johnson, LLD*. Edited by George Birkbeck Hill, revised by L. F. Powell. Clarendon Press.

Boswell, James (1950) *London Journal*. Edited by F. A. Pottle. Heinemann.

Bradley, Philip (1973) 'A long fiction index', *The Indexer* 8(3), April, 153–9.

Bradley, Philip (1989) 'Indexes to works of fiction: the views of producers and users on the need for them', *The Indexer* 16(4), October, 239–48.

Brett, Simon (1987) *The Faber book of diaries*. Faber and Faber, p. x.

Briggs, Julia (1990) Review of C. Williams' biography of Christina Stead, *The Times*, 27 January.

Bushrui, Suhil (1980) *Blue flame*. Longman.

Byatt, A. S. (1978) *The virgin in the garden*. Chatto & Windus, Chapter 21.

Byatt, A. S. (1986) *Still Life*. Penguin.

Byatt, A. S. (1990) *Possession*. Chatto & Windus.

Byatt, A. S. (1993) *Passions of the mind*. Virago, p. 17.

Byatt, A. S. (2001) Foreword to Hazel K. Bell, *Indexers and indexes in fact and fiction*. British Library/University of Toronto Press.

Campbell, Barry (2008) 'Politics as unusual; part three: sanity found', *The Walrus*, May, 75.

References

Carey, G. V. (1961) 'No room at the top', *The Indexer* **2**(4), Autumn, 120–3.

Carey, G. V. (1963) *Making an index*. Cambridge University Press, p. 6.

Cioffi, Frank (1998) *Wittgenstein on Freud and Frazer*. Cambridge University Press.

Cleveland, D. B. and Cleveland, Ana D. (1983) *Introduction to indexing and abstracting*. Libraries Unlimited, pp. 47, 148.

Collison, Robert (1962) 'On indexing a favourite novelist (Surtees)', *The Private Library* **4**(3), 42–4.

Cousins, Garry (2014) 'Society indexing awards', *The Indexer* **32**(1), 43–4.

Craine, Ian (2018) Letter, *The Indexer* **36**(4), 174.

de Beer, E. S. (1967) 'Dr. Powell's index to Boswell's *Life of Johnson*', *The Indexer* **5**(3), 135–9.

de Botton, Alain (1995) *Kiss & Tell*. Macmillan, pp. 10, 155.

Diamond, John (1992) 'A person's most significant decision', *The Times*, 15 May.

Drabble, Margaret (n.d.) 'Digging in the wild garden', lecture given to Centre for the Understanding of Society and Politics, Kingston University.

Edel, Leon (1984) *Writing lives, principia biographica*. Norton.

Ellis, Andrew (1992) 'Literary Indexes', *The Indexer* **18**(1), 50.

Fisk, Neil R. (1968) 'Indexing technical matter: some practical experience on both sides of two fences', *The Indexer* **6**(2), Autumn, 42–7.

Fitzgerald, Penelope (1998) 'So much to do', *Wall Street Journal*, 17 March, A16, 48.

Ford, Jill (1993) 'The Wheatley Medal: thirty years old: past, present and future', *The Indexer* **18**(3), 189–91.

Fox, Margalit (2013) 'Richard Ben Cramer, Writer of Big Ambitions, Dies at 62', *New York Times*, 8 January.

Gifford, Paul (2009) 'The ultimate French intellectual?', *TLS*, 11 March.

Glendinning, V. (2003) Review, *The Spectator*, 4 October.

Gordon, Giles (1993) Books, *Times Magazine*, 10 April.

Gordon, Michael (1983) 'Law and order, alphabetical', *The Indexer* **13**(4), October, 255–6.

Gottlieb, Laura Moss (1998) Wilson. Award Acceptance Speech. *Key Words* **6**(4), July/August, 15–17.

Greer, G. (2012) Review, *The Age*, 3 November.

Halliburton, Rachel (2000) 'New Writing 9', *TLS*, 24 March.

Halsband, Robert (1983) Review, *Times Literary Supplement*, 4 November.

Hamilton, Geoffrey (1976) 'How to recognise a good index', *The Indexer* **10**(2), 49–53.

Hardy, Thomas (1882) quoted in *The Life and Work of Thomas Hardy*, edited by Michael Millgate, Palgrave Macmillan, 1984, 156.

Hardy, Thomas (1874) *Far from the madding crowd*. Chapter 51.

Heiss, Anita (2015) 'Not all writers begin as readers', in D. Adelaide (ed.), *The Simple Act of Reading*. Vintage.

Hensher, Philip (2004) 'Dishonourable mentions', *The Independent*, 6 July 2004.

Heumann, Karl (1970) 'Diaries without indexes', *The Indexer* 7(2), Autumn, 90.

Hird, Barbara (2000) 'Colin Matthew 1941–1999', *The Indexer* **22**(1), April, 41.

Holmes, Richard (1997) 'Biography and Death', in A. L. Kennedy and John Fowles (eds), *New Writing 9*. Vintage, p. 390.

Holmstrom, Edwin (1965) 'The indexing of scientific books', *The Indexer* **4**(4), 123–31.

Imholtz, August A. (1996) *'Indexer nascitur, non fit*: Lewis Carroll as indexer again', *The Indexer* **20**(1), 11–13.

Indexing society awards (2016) *The Indexer* **34**(3), 125.

Irwin, Robert (2000) 'Your novel needs indexing', in A. L. Kennedy and John Fowles (eds), *New writing 9*. Vintage, p. 78.

ISO 999 (1996) *Information and documentation: Guidelines for the content, organization and presentation of indexes*. Geneva: International Organization for Standardization.

James, Robert Rhodes (1986) *Anthony Eden*. Weidenfeld & Nicolson.

Johnson, R. (2014) *Mail Online*, 16 March.

Knight, G. Norman (1964) *'Clemency' Canning*, *The Indexer* **4**(1), Spring, 19–20/29.

Knight, G. Norman (1966) 'Indexing the life of Sir Winston Churchill', *The Indexer* **5**(2), 58–63.

Knight, G. Norman (1970) 'The Wheatley Medal for 1969', *The Indexer* 7(2), Autumn, 57.

Knight, G. Norman (1979) *Indexing, the art of*. Allen & Unwin, p. 58.

Kramerae, C. (1985) *A Feminist Dictionary* by Cheris Kramerae and Paula Treichler. Pandora Press, p. 33.

Lancaster, F. W. (1991) *Indexing and abstracting in theory and practice*. Library Association Publishing, pp. 184–5, 189.

Laslett, Peter (1990) 'Editor and gent', *The Guardian*, October.

Latham, Robert (1984) 'The index to the definitive Pepys', *The Indexer* **14**(2), October, 88–90.

Latham, Robert, and Latham, Rosalind (1980) 'Indexing Pepys' diary', *The Indexer* **12**(1), April, 34–5.

Latham, R. C. and Matthews, W. (eds) (1983) *The diary of Samuel Pepys. Vol. XI Index*. Bell & Hyman.

Leacock, Stephen (1942) 'Index: there is no index', in *My remarkable uncle and other sketches*. Dodd, Mead & Company.

Lee, David (1991) 'Coping with a title: the indexer and the British aristocracy', *The Indexer* **17**(3), 155–60.

Lee, David (2001) 'Judging indexes: The criteria for a good index', *The Indexer* **22**(4), 191–4.

Lee, Jennifer (2004) 'Washington Books Bring Out Index Fingers', *New York Times*, 2 May.

Levin, Bernard (1983) Review, *The Observer*, 27 February.

Levin, Bernard (1989) 'Don't come to me for a reference', *The Times*, 10 November.

Lister, Michael (2006) Review, *Times Literary Supplement*, 21 July.

Lyons, John (1968) *Introduction to theoretical linguistics*. Cambridge University Press, p. 335.

Marris, G. Philip (2019) *Marris of Burton Corner*. G. Philip Marris.

Matthew, H. C. G. (1995) 'Indexing Gladstone: from 5 x 3" cards to computer and database', *The Indexer* **19**(4), 257–64.

Matthews, Douglas (1993) 'The tail and the dog: a book indexer speaks', *The Author*, Autumn, 90–1.

Matthews, Douglas (1996) 'Computerised indexing', *The Electronic Author*, Summer, 9–10.

Matthews, Douglas (1999) 'Broadcasting on indexing', *The Indexer* **21**(4), 172–3.

Matthews, Douglas (2001) 'Indexing published letters', *The Indexer* **22**(3), April, 135–41.

Matthews, Douglas (2004) 'Indexing Defoe', *The Indexer* **24**(1), April, 12–14.

McSmith, Andy (2011) Review, *The Oldie*, November 2011.

Muir, Hugh (2012) Diary, *The Guardian*, 21 June 2012.

Murphy, Tom (2003) 'Exploring fiction and poetry through indexing', *The Indexer* **23**(4), 216–17.

Orwell, George (1949) *Nineteen Eighty-four*. Secker & Warburg.

125

Phipps, Christopher (2006) 'Sterne stuff', *The Indexer* 25(2), 112–13.

Phipps, Christopher (2012) 'An indexer's life of Johnson', *The Indexer* 30(3), September, 114–19.

Phipps, Christopher (2017) 'Douglas Matthews at 90', *SIdelights* (4), 7.

Piggott, Mary (1991) 'Authors as their own indexers', *The Indexer* 17(3), April, 161–6.

Pym, Barbara (1985) *A Very Private Eye: The diaries, letters and notebooks of Barbara Pym*. Edited by Hazel Holt and Hilary Pym, Macmillan, 471–92.

Raven, Anthony (1990) 'Indexes to works of fiction' (letter), *The Indexer* 17(1), April, 60–1.

Ridehalgh, Nan (1985) 'The design of indexes', *The Indexer* 14(3), April, 165–74.

Roy, Kenneth (1993) in *Scotland on Sunday*, 5 September.

Sassen, Catherine (2012) 'Biography indexes reviewed', *The Indexer* 30(3), September, 138.

Sewell, Brian (2011) 'Brian Sewell's Art Books of the Year 2011', *Evening Standard*, 22 December.

Shaftesley, John M. (1972) Review, *The Indexer* 8(2), October, 125–8.

Simkin, John (1997) 'Professionalism', *The Indexer* 20(4), October, 178–81.

Singer, Peter (1977) *Animal liberation*. Granada Publishing, p. 14.

Spender, Dale (1986) *Scribbling sisters*. Camden Press.

Stauber, Do Mi (1998) 'A few comments from the chair of the judging committee', *Key Words* 6(4), 18.

Stauber, Do Mi (2004) *Facing the text: content and structure in book indexing*. Cedar Row Press.

Stern, Simon (2009) 'The case and the exceptions: creating instrumental texts in law and literature', in Laura L. Runge and Pat Rogers (eds), *Producing the eighteenth-century book: writers and publishers in England, 1650–1800*. University of Delaware Press, pp. 95–115.

Sutherland, John (2006) 'Indexing: a work of art or a sickness beyond cure?' *The Indexer* 25(1), 7–8.

Thornton, James C. (1965) 'How I indexed Dickens's letters', *The Indexer* 4(4), Autumn, 119–22.

Thornton, James C. (1968) 'The long index', in G. Norman Knight (ed.), *Training in indexing*. M.I.T. Press, pp. 86–96.

Toole, Wendy (2007) Book review, *The Indexer* 25(3), April, 221–2.

Towery, Margie (2017) 'Metatopic and structure', *The Indexer* 35(2), 72–4.

Tredell, Nicolas (1998) *Charles Dickens: Great Expectations*. Icon Books, p. 201.

Trubshaw, Bob (2005) '"A funny lot": indexing and local history books', *The Indexer* 24(4), 184–5.

Vickers, John A. (1991) 'Working in tandem: not forgetting the pc', *The Indexer* 17(4), October, 281–2.

Vonnegut, Kurt (1978) letter quoted in *The Indexer* 11(2), October, 103.

Wace, Michael (1975) in 'Awards for indexes', *The Indexer* 9(3), 107.

Walker, Alan (2012a) 'Political memoirs: an international comparison of indexing styles', *The Indexer* 30(2), 66–75.

Walker, Alan (2012b) 'Indexing political memoirs: neutrality and partiality', *The Indexer* 30(3), 125–30.

Weinberg, Bella Hass (1988) 'Why indexing fails the researcher', *The Indexer* 16(1), April, 3–6.

Weinberg, Bella Hass (1989) 'Indexing biographies' (letter), *The Indexer* 16(4), October, 279–80.

Wellisch, Hans H. (1991) *Indexing from A to Z*. H. W. Wilson, p. 243.

Wellisch, Hans H. (1992) 'Lewis Carroll as indexer', *The Indexer* 18(2), October, 110.

'The Wheatley Medal' (1970) *The Indexer* 7(2), 78.

Wheatley Medal (1992) *The Indexer* 18(1), April, 38.

Whittemore, Reed (1999) 'The Bio Biz', *The Wall Street Journal*, 1 October, W17.

Whorf, Benjamin Lee (1956) 'The relation of habitual thought and behaviour in language', in J. B. Carroll (ed.), *Language, thought and reality: selected writings*. MIT Press, pp. 134–59.

Wittmann, Cecelia (1990) 'Subheadings in award-winning book indexes: a quantitative evaluation', *The Indexer* 17(1) April, 3–6.

Woolf, Virginia (1932) 'I am Christina Rossetti', in *The second common reader*. Harcourt Brace, p. 237.

Woolf, Virginia (1939) 'A sketch of the past', in *Moments of Being*. Pimlico.

Wyman, L. Pilar (2001) 'SI/H.W. Wilson award for excellence in indexing, 2000', *Key Words* 9(4), July/August, 111–12.

Index

specialisms 6–7
Spectator, The 9
spelling 40
  variant 43, 114
Spender, Dale 56–7
  Women of ideas 57
Stalin, biography 23, 72
  names 42
standardization 58–9, 100
  editions of works 114
Standards 44, 48, 60, 106
Stauber, Do Mi
  on metatopic 78–9
  on Wilson Award winner 21–2
Stern, Simon 111
Sterne, Laurence
  Tristram Shandy 118
strings 18–19, 90–5
  articles on, listed 95
  see also minor mentions
subheadings 2, 30, 32, 76–7, 79, 90,
  91
  in Arnold letters 15
  arrangement 32, 60–7
    alphabetical 60, 63, 66–7,
      78
    chronological 61, 63–5, 92,
      97–8
    page-order 60, 61–3
    thematic 68–74
  in award-winning indexes, study
    24, 44, 46, 97–8
  blocks 65
  bracketed 91–2, 98
  in fiction 115
  in histories 4, 44, 46, 61, 64
  letters 89
  and minor mentions 90–4

setting
  indented 97, 99
  run-on 97–8
  terminology 44–9, 55, 66–7
  impartiality 51–4
  thesauri 58
  written works 86–7
  see also paragraphed subheadings
subject specialism 6–7
sub-subheadings 68, 70, 73
  in Austen biography 89
  in Carlyle biography 80
  in Connolly biography 81–2
  in Pepys diary 101
  in run–on layout 98
Surtees, Robert Smith, novels
  112
Sutherland, John 113
symbols 60, 96
  in fiction 110, 114
  typographic 104

teaching, indexing as 29, 112
terminology 1, 44–50
  assigned 45
  derived 45
  impartiality 51–4
Thatcher, Margaret, biography 7
thematic grouping of subheadings 61,
  68–73, 112–13
themes 2, 6, 32, 68, 93, 110
  echoing 93
  in fiction 114
    extended by index 113
  in letters 13, 14
  tracing 73–4, 79
thesauri 58
Thirkell, Angela, novels 110, 119